celebrating
CHOCOLATE
CAKES, BROWNIES & BARS

By

Avner Laskin

A LEISURE ARTS PUBLICATION

President and Chief Executive Officer: Rick Barton
Vice President and Chief Operations Officer: Tom Siebenmorgen
Vice President of Sales: Mike Behar
Director of Finance and Administration: Laticia Mull Dittrich
National Sales Director: Martha Adams
Creative Services: Chaska Lucas
Information Technology Director: Hermine Linz
Controller: Francis Caple
Vice President, Operations: Jim Dittrich
Retail Customer Service Manager: Stan Raynor
Print Production Manager: Fred F. Pruss
Editor-in-Chief: Susan White Sullivan
Director of Designer Relations: Cheryl Johnson
Special Projects Director: Susan Frantz Wiles
Art Publications Director: Rhonda Shelby
Senior Prepress Director: Mark Hawkins

Produced for Leisure Arts, Inc. by Penn Publishing Ltd.
www.penn.co.il
Editor: Deanna Linder
Culinary editing: Tamar Zakut
Design and layout: Ariane Rybski
Photography by: Daniel Lailah
Food styling: Amit Farber

PRINTED IN CHINA

ISBN-13: 978-1-60900-115-5
Library of Congress Control Number: 2010941076

Cover photography by Daniel Lailah

Contents

Introduction

Yes, I am addicted to chocolate; the unsweetened, quality kind. I bake with chocolate, make drinks with chocolate, and use chocolate in savory dishes as well. I enjoy quality chocolate to celebrate happy times, or when I just need some comfort food.

I am delighted to have read about recent studies that prove that chocolate and its main ingredient, cacao, contain nutrients such as antioxidants that are rich in magnesium, calcium, iron and zinc, along with other essential nutrients. Of course, that doesn't mean that you should eat an unlimited amount of chocolate, but it does mean that when you eat chocolate, it should be quality chocolate with a high percentage of cacao.

As you will see throughout this book, I prefer to use unsweetened chocolate, but you can always use milk chocolate instead, using the same amounts as listed.

Chocolate works on all the senses, not just on your taste buds. Chocolate symbolizes love, passion, celebration and comfort. It is even used in the field of cosmetics.

Up until the 16th century, cacao was cultivated only by the Aztecs and the Incas in South America. It wasn't until the middle of the 16th century that cacao beans became available in Europe through trade and even then they were only available to the very rich because they were very costly. In the beginning, cacao was consumed only in liquid form and it took years until people began consuming the solid form that we know today.

Chocolate can be made from three different varieties of cacao beans, differentiated by their aroma and bitterness. The beans are cultivated, dried and wrapped in banana leaves until fermented and then they are shipped to the various chocolate manufacturers around the globe. The manufacturers roast and grind the chocolate until it becomes a liquid extract, made of 50% cacao butter and 50% cacao solids. The chocolate is then made into bars and additional ingredients, such as sugar, palm oil, milk, cocoa powder, etc. are added until finally, the cacao butter is removed. The quality of chocolate is measured by the percentage of cacao solids remaining in the final product.

In this book you will find recipes for cakes, bars and brownies, all of which contain chocolate as their main ingredient. Some of the recipes are quite traditional, while others are more innovative. Some of the recipes are quick and easy, whereas others take more time and effort to prepare.

All the recipes you will find in this book are tried and tested. Only after I had successfully prepared them in my home kitchen did they make it to the pages of this book. It's very important to read through the tips and to read each recipe through before starting to prepare it. Make sure you have all the ingredients and the proper tools at hand. Also make sure you have enough time to make the recipe. That way the success of the recipe is guaranteed.

I hope you enjoy this book as much as we did making it.

Avner Laskin

Cakes

Chocolate Donuts • Black Forest Cake •

Devil's Food Cake • German Chocolate Cake •

Tunnel of Fudge Cake • Chocolate Orange Pound Cake •

Chocolate Marble Cake • Chocolate Babka Cake •

Chocolate Cheesecake • Cold Chocolate Tart •

Chocolate Pound Cake • Kid's Chocolate Cake •

Double Chocolate Roll Cake • Chocolate Angel Food Cake •

Chocolate Chip and Pistachio Cake • Chocolate Napoleon Cake •

Chocolate Mascarpone Cake • Chocolate Mocha Cream Cake •

Baked Chocolate Tart • Death by Chocolate Cake •

Chocolate Ricotta Cheese Cake • Chocolate Poppy Seed Cake •

Chocolate Prune Cake • Chocolate Brioche Cake •

Steamed Chocolate Cake • Chocolate Meringue Cake •

Hot Chocolate Cake • Molten Chocolate Cake •

Double Chocolate Cake • Chocolate Almond Torte •

Baked Chocolate Mousse Cake • Chocolate Charlotte Cake •

Chocolate Donuts

25

This recipe will make you never want to buy store-bought donuts again. Make the cream filling a day in advance (and keep in the refrigerator). By doing so, you'll have your fresh donuts quicker than if you went to buy them at the store!

INGREDIENTS

For the dough

1 tablespoon fresh yeast

¼ cup water, at room temperature

1 egg

3 tablespoons sugar

2 cups all-purpose flour

1 teaspoon salt

¼ stick (2 oz.) butter, softened

For the filling

¾ cup heavy cream

¾ cup powdered sugar

6 oz. unsweetened chocolate

1 tablespoon pure vanilla extract

For frying

2 pounds canola oil or sunflower oil

For decorating

2 tablespoons powdered sugar

PREPARATION

1. Using a mixer fitted with a hook attachment, mix together the yeast, water, egg, sugar and flour on low speed for 3 minutes. Increase mixer speed to medium, add the salt and butter, and continue to mix for 5 minutes.

2. Transfer dough to a lightly floured bowl and place in the refrigerator for 1 hour.

3. Meanwhile, prepare the filling: Place the heavy cream and powdered sugar in a medium saucepan over medium heat and cook until just boiling. Remove from heat, add the chocolate and vanilla extract, and use a whisk to stir until the chocolate has melted and the mixture is combined. Transfer mixture to a bowl and freeze for 20 minutes.

4. Remove dough from refrigerator and divide dough evenly into 8 equal pieces. Working on a lightly floured surface, roll each piece into a ball and let them rest for 10 minutes.

5. Place the dough balls onto a clean work surface, covered by a lightly floured kitchen towel and let them rise for 1 hour, until they have doubled in size.

6. Once the dough balls have risen, heat the oil in a large saucepan on medium heat until it reaches about 350°F. Fry each ball for about 3 minutes until golden. Once fried, place each ball on paper towels, to soak up some of the remaining oil. Allow donuts to cool for 15 minutes.

7. Transfer the filling to a piping bag fitted with a round tip and pipe the filling into the middle of the top of each donut. Decorate with powdered sugar and serve immediately.

Black Forest Cake

Serves

12

This cake gets its name from the mountain range in south-western Germany and is distinctive by virtue of its chocolate cake layers, smothered in chocolate mousse and cherries.

INGREDIENTS

For the cake

4 eggs, yolks and whites separated

⅔ cup sugar

½ cup all-purpose flour

3 tablespoons cocoa powder

For the chocolate mousse filling

4 cups heavy cream

12 oz. unsweetened chocolate, cut into small cubes

2 cups fresh cherries, pitted

2 tablespoons cherry liqueur, or any other fruit liqueur

PREPARATION

1. Preheat oven to 350°F.

2. Using a mixer fitted with a whisk attachment, whisk the egg whites on high speed for about 5 minutes, until light and fluffy. Gradually add half the sugar and continue to whisk until glossy, white peaks form. Transfer egg whites to a clean, dry bowl.

3. Clean and dry the mixer bowl. Using a mixer fitted with a whisk attachment, whisk the egg yolks and the remaining sugar on high speed for 5 minutes, until light and fluffy. Gradually add the flour and cocoa powder.

4. Using a rubber spatula, gently fold the egg yolk mixture into the egg whites, until combined. Transfer mixture to a piping bag fitted with a round tip.

5. Place a sheet of parchment paper onto a baking sheet and pipe two 12-inch by 4-inch rectangles onto the sheet.

6. Bake for 22 minutes. Allow to cool on a cooling rack for 30 minutes, until they reach room temperature.

7. Meanwhile, prepare the chocolate mousse filling: Place one cup of the heavy cream into a small saucepan over medium heat and cook until just boiling. Remove from heat and add chocolate. Use a whisk to stir until chocolate is melted and the mixture is smooth. Set aside for later use.

8. Place the cherries and cherry liqueur in a small bowl and allow the cherries to marinate for 30 minutes.

(continued on page 12)

(continued from page 10)

9. Using a mixer fitted with a whisk attachment, whisk the remaining heavy cream on high speed for about 8 minutes, until firm. Use a rubber spatula to fold in the prepared chocolate filling, until combined. Transfer mousse to a piping bag fitted with a round tip.

10. Assemble the cake: Place one of the prepared cake rectangles onto a large serving plate. Pipe a layer of the mousse filling onto the cake, starting from the edges and finishing in the center. Place half the marinated cherries evenly onto the mousse. Place the cake in the freezer for 30 minutes.

11. Remove cake from the freezer and place the second cake rectangle on top of the cherries. Pipe in the remaining mousse filling and top with the remaining marinated cherries. Place cake in the freezer for at least 2 hours, preferably overnight, before serving.

12. Cake may be stored in the refrigerator for up to 2 days.

Devil's Food Cake

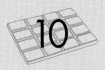

This moist and airy cake will become a staple in your
cake-making repertoire.

INGREDIENTS

For the cake

1½ cups all-purpose flour

½ cup cocoa powder

1¼ teaspoons baking soda

¼ teaspoon salt

1 cup sugar

1 cup sweet condensed milk

⅔ cup canola oil

1 teaspoon pure vanilla extract

For the cream frosting

3 oz. unsweetened chocolate

1 stick (4 oz.) butter

⅓ cup cocoa powder

2 tablespoons powdered sugar

½ tablespoon pure vanilla extract

⅔ cup sour cream

PREPARATION

1. Preheat oven to 325°F. Butter and lightly flour two round
8-inch cake pans.

2. In a large bowl, mix together the flour, cocoa powder,
baking soda and salt.

3. Using a stand mixer fitted with a whisk attachment, whisk
together the sugar, sweetened condensed milk, canola oil
and vanilla extract on low speed and gradually add the dry
ingredients. Whisk together until all ingredients are well
combined and the mixture is smooth.

4. Divide the mixture evenly into the two prepared cake pans.
Bake for 35 minutes or until a toothpick inserted comes out
clean. Allow to cool on a cooling rack for 1 hour.

5. Prepare the frosting: Melt chocolate in a heatproof bowl,
set over a pan of simmering water. Stir occasionally. Add
the butter and stir until butter is incorporated. Remove
from heat, gradually add the cocoa powder and mix until
combined. Add the powdered sugar and mix until combined.
Add the vanilla extract and sour cream, and continue to stir
until all ingredients are combined and the mixture is smooth.

6. Assemble the cake: Place one of the cakes on a large
serving plate. Using an offset spatula, spread ⅓ of the
frosting onto the cake. Cover the frosting with the second
prepared cake. Use the remaining frosting to cover both
the top and the sides of the cake. Refrigerate cake at least
2 hours before serving.

7. Cake can be stored in the refrigerator for up to 2 days.

German Chocolate Cake

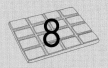

Serves

8

Contrary to popular belief, this cake did not originate in Germany. The original recipe can be traced back to 1852, when an Englishman developed a brand of dark baking chocolate. The Englishman's name was Sam German and the product, Baker's German's Sweet Chocolate, was named after him.

INGREDIENTS

For the cake

2½ cups cake flour

1 teaspoon baking soda

½ teaspoon salt

5 oz. unsweetened chocolate

½ cup boiling water

2 sticks (8 oz.) butter

1½ cups sugar

1 teaspoon pure vanilla extract

5 eggs, yolks and whites separated

1 cup sweet condensed milk

For the frosting

1 cup milk

1 cup sugar

3 egg yolks

1 teaspoon pure vanilla extract

1 stick (4 oz.) butter

1½ cups shredded coconut

1 cup roasted pecans, coarsely chopped

PREPARATION

1. Preheat oven to 325°F. Butter three round 8-inch silicon or Teflon cake pans.

2. In a medium bowl, mix together the cake flour, baking soda and salt.

3. Place the chocolate and boiling water in a medium bowl and use a whisk to mix, until the ingredients are combined and the mixture is smooth. Set aside for later use.

4. Using a mixer fitted with a whisk attachment, mix together the butter and 1 cup of sugar on medium speed for 2 minutes, until the mixture is smooth. Add the egg yolks (one at a time) and continue to mix on medium speed until yolks are incorporated. Add the chocolate and vanilla extract and continue to mix for another 2 minutes, until all ingredients are incorporated.

5. Alternately add the condensed milk and the flour mixture, until both ingredients are well combined. Transfer prepared batter to a large bowl and set aside for later use.

6. Clean and dry mixer bowl. Using a mixer fitted with a whisk attachment, whisk the egg whites on high speed for 7 minutes. Gradually add the remaining ½ cup of sugar and continue to whisk on high speed until glossy white peaks form.

7. Using a rubber spatula, fold the egg whites into the prepared batter and fold until the batter is combined.

(continued on page 16)

(continued from page 14)

8. Divide the mixture evenly into the three prepared cake pans. Bake for 38 minutes or until a toothpick inserted comes out clean. Allow to cool on a cooling rack for 1 hour.

9. Prepare the frosting: Place the milk, sugar, egg yolks, vanilla extract and butter in a small saucepan over medium heat and using a whisk, constantly stir for 8 minutes until the butter has melted. Add the coconut and pecans and continue whisking for another 5 minutes, and then remove from heat. Allow frosting to cool to room temperature before using.

10. Assemble the cake: Place one of the cakes on a large serving plate. Using an offset spatula, spread a layer of the frosting onto the cake. Cover frosting with the second prepared cake. Spread another layer of the frosting onto the cake. Top with the third prepared cake and place the cake in the freezer for 30 minutes.

11. Remove cake from freezer and use the remaining frosting to cover both the top and the sides of the cake. Refrigerate cake at least 1 hour before serving.

12. Cake can be stored in the refrigerator for up to 2 days.

Tunnel of Fudge Cake

16

This cake has a soft fudgy inside and chocolate frosting outside. It is the perfect recipe for the ultimate chocolate lover.

INGREDIENTS

For the cake

1¾ cups sugar

3¼ sticks (13 oz.) butter, softened

6 eggs

2 cups powdered sugar

2½ cups all-purpose flour

½ cup cocoa powder

For the frosting

¼ cup milk, warm

1 cup powdered sugar

⅓ cup cocoa powder

PREPARATION

1. Preheat oven to 325°F. Butter a 12-cup fluted tube pan.

2. Using a mixer fitted with a whisk attachment, whisk together the sugar and butter on medium speed for 4 minutes, until light and fluffy. Add the eggs (one at a time) and continue to whisk for another 2 minutes. Reduce mixer speed, add the powdered sugar, flour and cocoa powder, and continue to mix for another 2 minutes until all ingredients are incorporated.

3. Pour the mixture evenly into prepared pan and bake for 50 minutes. Allow cake to cool on a cooling rack for 2 hours.

4. After 2 hours, carefully release the cake onto a serving plate. Place the cake in the refrigerator for at least 2 hours, preferably overnight, before frosting.

5. Prepare the frosting: In a medium bowl, use a whisk to mix together the milk, powdered sugar and cocoa powder until the mixture is smooth.

6. Remove cake from refrigerator and pour the frosting evenly over the entire cake, so that it drips down the sides. Place cake in the freezer for 15 minutes before serving.

7. Cake can be stored in the refrigerator for up to 3 days.

Chocolate Orange Pound Cake

The combination of orange and chocolate works wonders with this already classic pound cake.

INGREDIENTS

For graham cracker crust

2 sticks (8 oz.) butter, softened

1⅔ cups sugar

½ cup brown sugar, packed

1 teaspoon orange zest

6 eggs

2⅔ cups flour

1 cup sweet condensed milk

2 tablespoons orange liqueur

1 tablespoon pure vanilla extract

½ teaspoon baking soda

½ teaspoon baking powder

¾ cup good quality cocoa powder

For the syrup

⅓ cup water

½ cup sugar

2 tablespoons orange liqueur

PREPARATION

1. Preheat oven to 325°F. Butter and lightly flour an 8-inch by 4-inch loaf pan.

2. Using a mixer fitted with a whisk attachment, mix together the butter, both sugars, and orange zest on medium speed for 4 minutes. Add the eggs (one at a time) and half the flour, and continue mixing for 3 minutes. Add the condensed milk, orange liqueur, vanilla extract, baking soda, baking powder, cocoa powder and the remaining flour and continue mixing for 3 minutes. Allow mixture to rest for 15 minutes.

3. Pour the mixture evenly into the prepared pan and bake for 1 hour.

4. Meanwhile, make the syrup: Place the water and sugar in a small saucepan over medium heat, cook until just boiling and then remove from heat. Add the orange liqueur and mix. Set aside until cake is baked.

5. Remove the baked cake from the oven and immediately pour the syrup over the cake. Allow cake to cool on a cooling rack for 30 minutes before serving.

6. Cake can be stored in an airtight container at room temperature for up to 2 days.

Chocolate Marble Cake

Serves

12

Marble cake provides the best of both worlds; for vanilla lovers and chocolate lovers alike.

INGREDIENTS

6 oz. unsweetened chocolate

2 sticks (8 oz.) butter, softened

1½ cups sugar

1 cup milk

2½ cups all-purpose flour

½ cup sour cream

3 eggs

1 teaspoon baking powder

1 tablespoon pure vanilla extract

PREPARATION

1. Preheat oven to 325°F. Butter and lightly flour an 8-inch by 4-inch loaf pan.

2. Melt chocolate and half the butter in a heatproof bowl, and set over a pan of simmering water. Stir occasionally until chocolate has completely melted and the mixture is smooth. Remove from heat and set aside for later use.

3. Using a mixer fitted with a whisk attachment, mix the remaining butter with the sugar on medium speed for 4 minutes. Add the milk and half the flour, and continue whisking for an additional 3 minutes. Add the sour cream, eggs, baking powder, vanilla extract and the remaining flour, and continue whisking for 3 minutes.

4. Pour ⅓ of the mixture into a small bowl. Pour the remaining mixture into a separate bowl.

5. Using a whisk, mix the melted chocolate into the bowl with ⅓ of the mixture, until it is well combined.

6. Pour half of the "white" mixture into the prepared pan and then pour half of the chocolate mixture on top. Pour the remaining "white" mixture on top of the chocolate mixture, and then pour the remaining chocolate mixture on top.

7. Using a knife or a wooden skewer, move through batter in a figure-eight motion to create swirls. Bake for 55 minutes. Allow cake to cool on a cooling rack for 30 minutes before serving.

8. Cake can be stored in an airtight container at room temperature for up to 2 days.

Chocolate Babka Cake

Serves

12

The Babka cake is a spongy yeast cake that is traditionally baked for Easter Sunday in Eastern European countries, such as Poland, Lithuania and Latvia.

INGREDIENTS

For the dough

2 tablespoons fresh yeast

½ cup water, at room temperature

1 egg

3 tablespoons sugar

2½ cups all-purpose flour

1 teaspoon salt

1½ sticks (6 oz.) butter, softened

For the filling

2 sticks (8 oz.) butter, softened

¾ cup powdered sugar

3 tablespoons good quality cocoa powder

1 tablespoon pure vanilla extract

1 egg, beaten (for brushing)

PREPARATION

1. Using a mixer fitted with a hook attachment, mix together the yeast, water, egg, sugar and flour on low speed for 3 minutes.

2. Add the salt and butter and continue mixing on medium speed for 5 minutes. Transfer dough to a lightly floured bowl and place in the refrigerator for 1 hour.

3. Preheat oven to 350°F and butter a 12-cup fluted tube pan.

4. Using a mixer fitted with a whisk attachment, mix together all the ingredients for the filling (excluding the beaten egg) on low speed for 3 minutes, until all ingredients are well combined and mixture is smooth. Set aside for later use.

5. Remove dough from refrigerator and working on a lightly floured surface, evenly divide the dough into two pieces. Use a rolling pin to roll each piece of dough into a 12-inch by 5-inch rectangle, ⅛-inch thick. Brush half of the filling onto one rolled-out piece. Repeat by brushing the remaining filling onto the second piece. Gently roll each piece lengthwise. Braid both of the pieces together and secure both sides by pinching them together.

6. Place the dough into the prepared pan and brush with the beaten egg. Allow the dough to rise in a dry, warm place for 1½ hours, until it has tripled in size.

7. Bake for 35 minutes. Allow to cool on a cooling rack until reaching room temperature before serving.

8. Cake may be stored in an airtight container at room temperature for 1 day.

Chocolate Cheesecake

Serves

10

Your favorite cheesecake just got upgraded by adding a much needed dose of chocolate.

INGREDIENTS

For graham cracker crust

1¼ cups graham cracker crumbs

½ stick (2 oz.) butter, softened

1 tablespoon good quality cocoa powder

For the cake

6 oz. unsweetened chocolate

2 cups cream cheese

1 teaspoon pure vanilla extract

1 cup sugar

3 egg yolks + 3 eggs

¾ cup sour cream

2 tablespoons good quality cocoa powder

PREPARATION

1. Preheat oven to 325°F and butter a round 10-inch springform pan.

2. Place all the ingredients for the crust into a food processor and stir until the mixture is combined.

3. Turn the crust mixture into the prepared springform pan and use your fingers to pat an even layer of crumbs over the bottom of the pan. Place the pan in the freezer until further use.

4. Melt chocolate in a large heatproof bowl, set over a pan of simmering water. Stir occasionally until chocolate has melted completely. Set aside and allow to cool.

5. Using a mixer fitted with a whisk attachment, mix the cream cheese and vanilla extract on low speed for 2-3 minutes, until the cream cheese is smooth. Increase mixer speed to medium and gradually add the sugar, mixing until all the sugar is combined. Add the egg yolks, then add the eggs (one at a time) and whisk until combined. Add the sour cream and whisk for an additional 2 minutes. Add the cocoa powder and whisk for another minute, until all ingredients are incorporated.

6. Add ⅓ of the cream cheese mixture into the bowl with the melted chocolate and use a whisk to stir until the mixture is smooth. Fold in the remaining cream cheese mixture using a rubber spatula.

7. Remove pan from freezer and pour the mixture evenly onto the crust. Bake for 45 minutes. Allow cheesecake to cool to room temperature on a cooking rack before removing from pan.

8. Cake may be stored in an airtight container in the refrigerator for up to 2 days.

Cold Chocolate Tart

4

The combination of crispy tart dough and creamy chocolate filling will ensure that not much of this cake is left over.

INGREDIENTS

For the crust

2 sticks (8 oz.) butter, cold

¼ cup powdered sugar

1 egg + 1 egg, beaten

1 tablespoon cold water

½ teaspoon salt

2½ cups all-purpose flour

For the filling

12 oz. unsweetened chocolate

1 cup heavy cream

1 tablespoon brandy

For decoration

¼ cup unsweetened chocolate, grated

PREPARATION

1. Make the crust: Place the butter and sugar in a food processor and mix for 2 minutes, wiping down the sides, until the mixture is smooth. Add the egg, water and salt, and continue mixing for another 2 minutes until all ingredients are combined. Add the flour and mix for another minute until dough is formed.

2. Remove ball of dough, wrap in plastic wrap and refrigerate for at least 1 hour before using.

3. Preheat oven to 350°F.

4. Working on a lightly floured surface, roll out the dough to ⅛-inch thick. Cut out four 4-inch circles from the dough and place each piece into an individual 4-inch tart dish. Using your fingers, press the dough to the sides of the dish so that it adheres. Place the dishes in the refrigerator for 15 minutes.

5. Cut four 4-inch circles out of parchment paper and place one into each tart dish, on top of the dough. Fill the dishes with dried beans or baking weights and bake for 20 minutes.

6. Remove dishes from oven and carefully remove the parchment paper, along with the dried beans or baking weights. Brush the crust with the beaten egg and bake again for another 3 minutes.

(continued on page 28)

[continued from page 26]

7. Remove dishes from oven and allow them to cool on a cooling rack until reaching room temperature.

8. Make the filling: Melt the chocolate and heavy cream in a heatproof bowl, set over a pan of simmering water. Stir occasionally until chocolate has completely melted and the mixture is smooth. Remove from heat and add the brandy.

9. Pour the chocolate filling evenly into each tart dish and freeze for at least 1 hour.

10. Remove from freezer and decorate with grated chocolate shavings. Serve immediately.

11. Tart may be stored in an airtight container in the refrigerator for up to 2 days.

Chocolate Pound Cake

Traditionally, pound cake was made with a pound of each of four ingredients: flour, butter, eggs and sugar. The traditional recipe makes a cake much bigger than what the typical family can consume. Try this scaled down, chocolate version. Your family will thank you.

INGREDIENTS

For the cake

¼ cup sugar + 2½ cups sugar

2 cups all-purpose flour

1 teaspoon baking powder

1 teaspoon baking soda

1 cup cocoa powder

3 sticks (12 oz.) butter, softened

1 cup sweet condensed milk

6 eggs

1 tablespoon pure vanilla extract

2 tablespoons instant coffee (dissolved in 2 tablespoons boiling water)

For decoration

Powdered sugar

PREPARATION

1. Preheat oven to 325°F. Butter a 10-inch Bundt pan and coat with ¼ cup of sugar.

2. In a large bowl, mix together the flour, baking powder, baking soda and cocoa powder.

3. Using a mixer fitted with a paddle attachment, mix together the butter, condensed milk and the 2½ cups sugar on medium speed for 4 minutes, until light and fluffy. Add the eggs (one at a time) and continue mixing until all the eggs are combined. Add the vanilla extract and instant coffee, and mix for another 2 minutes until the mixture is smooth.

4. Reduce mixer speed and gradually add the dry ingredients. Once all the dry ingredients have been added, mix for another 30 seconds until the mixture is smooth.

5. Pour the mixture evenly into the prepared pan and bake for 1 hour, until a toothpick inserted comes out clean. Allow to cool on a cooling rack for 40 minutes.

6. Carefully remove cake from pan and place on a serving plate. Decorate with the desired amount of powdered sugar and serve.

7. Cake can be stored in an airtight container at room temperature for up to 2 days.

Kid's Chocolate Cake

Serves

12

The perfect chocolate cake that every child adores, this cake will become a staple for every birthday party. Mix it up each year by changing the decoration.

INGREDIENTS

For the cake

7 oz. good quality unsweetened chocolate

1½ sticks (6 oz.) butter

6 eggs

1 cup sugar

¾ cup all-purpose flour

For the frosting

½ cup heavy cream

2 tablespoons sugar

5 oz. unsweetened chocolate

PREPARATION

1. Preheat oven to 350°F and butter a round 10-inch springform pan.

2. Melt chocolate and butter in a heatproof bowl, set over a pan of simmering water. Stir occasionally until chocolate has completely melted and the mixture is smooth. Remove from heat.

3. Using a mixer fitted with a whisk attachment, whisk together the eggs and sugar on medium speed for about 7 minutes, until light and fluffy.

4. Using a rubber spatula, fold the flour into the chocolate mixture until combined, and then fold the chocolate mixture into the egg mixture until all ingredients are incorporated.

5. Pour the mixture into the prepared pan and bake for 30 minutes. Allow the cake to cool on a cooling rack for 30 minutes.

6. Prepare the frosting: Place the heavy cream and sugar into a small saucepan over medium heat and cook until just boiling. Remove from heat and add chocolate. Use a whisk to stir until chocolate is melted and the mixture is smooth.

7. Assemble the cake: Place a large plate underneath the cooling rack with the cake on it. Pour the frosting evenly over the cake. Freeze cake for 30 minutes and serve immediately.

8. Cake may be stored in an airtight container in the refrigerator for up to 3 days.

Double Chocolate Roll

Serves

12

This cake takes some time to make, so it's perfect for that cold weekend when you are snuggling up at home with the family.

INGREDIENTS

For the dough

1 tablespoon fresh yeast

¼ cup water, at room temperature

1 egg

2 tablespoons sugar

1¾ cups all-purpose flour

½ teaspoon salt

½ stick (2 oz.) butter, softened

For the chocolate roll filling

1 stick (4 oz.) butter, softened

½ cup powdered sugar

2 tablespoons good quality cocoa powder

½ tablespoon pure vanilla extract

For the cake filling

6 oz. good quality unsweetened chocolate

1½ sticks (6 oz.) butter

5 eggs

1 cup sugar

2 tablespoons cocoa powder

½ cup all-purpose flour

PREPARATION

1. Butter a 12-cup fluted tube pan.

2. Using a mixer fitted with a hook attachment, mix together the yeast, water, egg, sugar and flour on low speed for 3 minutes. Increase mixer speed to medium, add the salt and butter, and continue to mix for 5 minutes.

3. Transfer dough to a lightly floured bowl and place in the refrigerator for 1 hour.

4. Meanwhile, prepare the chocolate roll filling: Using a mixer fitted with a whisk attachment, mix together the butter, powdered sugar, cocoa powder and vanilla extract on low speed for 3 minutes, until all ingredients are combined and mixture is smooth. Set aside for later use.

5. Remove dough from refrigerator. Working on a lightly floured surface, use a rolling pin to roll out the dough into a 12-inch by 5-inch rectangle, ⅛-inch thick. Brush the filling onto the rolled-out dough. Gently roll the dough lengthwise and use a sharp knife to cut the roll into 6 equal pieces.

6. Place the pieces into the prepared pan and brush with the beaten egg. Allow the dough to rise in a dry, warm place for 1½ hours, until it has tripled in size.

7. Preheat oven to 350°F.

(continued on page 34)

(continued from page 32)

8. Meanwhile, prepare the cake filling: Melt the chocolate and butter in a heatproof bowl, set over a pan of simmering water. Stir occasionally until chocolate has completely melted and the mixture is smooth. Remove from heat and set aside.

9. Using a mixer fitted with a whisk attachment, whisk together the eggs and sugar on medium speed for about 7 minutes, until light and fluffy.

10. Using a rubber spatula, fold the cocoa powder and flour into the chocolate mixture until combined, and then fold the chocolate mixture into the egg mixture until all ingredients are incorporated.

11. Pour the mixture into the pan with the risen chocolate rolls, so that it sets in between each roll (but doesn't cover them). Bake for 10 minutes. Reduce oven temperature to 325°F and continue baking for another 40 minutes. Allow the cake to cool on a cooling rack for 40 minutes before serving.

12. Cake may be stored in an airtight container at room temperature for 1 day.

Chocolate Angel Food Cake

12

Angel food cake is a type of sponge cake that originated in North America. It gets its name from its airy lightness, said to be the "food of the angels".

INGREDIENTS

For the cake

1½ cups powdered sugar

1¼ cups all-purpose flour

¼ cup cocoa powder

2 cups egg whites (from about 16 eggs)

1 tablespoon cream of tartar

1½ cups sugar

1 tablespoon pure vanilla extract

For the frosting

1 cup powdered sugar

½ cup heavy cream, warm

¼ cup cocoa powder

PREPARATION

1. Preheat oven to 325° and butter a 12-cup fluted tube pan.

2. In a large bowl, mix together the powdered sugar, flour and cocoa powder, until all ingredients are combined.

3. Using a mixer fitted with a whisk attachment, mix the egg whites on high speed for about 7 minutes until glossy, white peaks form. Once firm, add the cream of tartar and continue whisking. Gradually add the sugar, and then add the vanilla extract.

4. Transfer whipped cream to a large bowl. Using a rubber spatula, gradually fold the dry ingredients into the egg whites mixture, until all ingredients are combined and the mixture is smooth.

5. Pour the mixture evenly into the prepared pan and bake for 1 hour. Allow cake to cool on a cooling rack for 2 hours.

6. Meanwhile, prepare the frosting: Place the heavy cream and powdered sugar in a bowl. Using a whisk, stir the two ingredients together, until smooth. Add the cocoa and continue to whisk until combined. Set aside until the cake has completely cooled.

7. Carefully remove the cake from the pan and set on a serving plate. Pour the frosting evenly over the top of the cake, allowing it to drip down over the sides. Place cake in the freezer for 10 minutes and then serve.

8. Cake can be stored in an airtight container in the refrigerator for up to 2 days.

Chocolate Chip and Pistachio Cake

Serves

12

This cake is a cinch to make and is perfect to make as a quick dessert when those last-minute guests arrive.

INGREDIENTS

2 sticks (8 oz.) butter, softened

1 cup sugar

$\frac{1}{2}$ cup dark brown sugar

3 eggs

$\frac{3}{4}$ cup pistachios, coarsely chopped

$1\frac{1}{3}$ cups all-purpose flour

2 teaspoons baking powder

3 tablespoons cocoa powder

$\frac{1}{2}$ cup chocolate chips

PREPARATION

1. Preheat oven to 340°F. Butter an 8-inch by 4-inch loaf pan.

2. Using a mixer fitted with a whisk attachment, mix together the butter and both sugars on medium speed for 2 minutes until the mixture is smooth.

3. Reduce mixer speed to low, add the eggs, pistachios, flour, baking powder and cocoa powder, and continue to mix for another 3 minutes until all ingredients are combined.

4. Using a wooden spoon or rubber spatula, stir in the chocolate chips. Pour the mixture into the prepared pan and bake for 35 minutes or until a toothpick inserted comes out clean. Allow to cool on a cooling rack for 1 hour.

5. Cake may be stored in an airtight container at room temperature for up to 2 days.

Chocolate Napoleon Cake

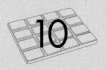

In this recipe you make your own-home made puff pastry. If you don't have the time, you can use store-bought puff pastry.

INGREDIENTS

For the puff pastry

½ cup water

1 teaspoon salt

½ stick (2 oz.) butter, melted + 2 sticks (8 oz.) butter, cold (for folding)

¼ cup powdered sugar

1⅔ cups all-purpose flour

3 tablespoons cocoa powder

For the chocolate cream filling

1 cup heavy cream

¼ cup powdered sugar

10 oz. unsweetened chocolate

1 tablespoon pure vanilla extract

For decoration

Cocoa powder

Powdered sugar

PREPARATION

1. Using a mixer fitted with a hook attachment, mix together the water, salt, melted butter, powdered sugar, flour and cocoa powder on low speed for 4 minutes. The dough will be lumpy and not smooth. Place the dough in the refrigerator for 30 minutes.

2. Meanwhile, prepare the butter for folding: Cover the butter with parchment paper and use a rolling pin to gently roll it out into a 6-inch square.

3. Once the dough is ready, remove it from the refrigerator. Working on a lightly floured surface, use a rolling pin to roll out the dough into a 10-inch circle. Place the butter square (parchment paper removed) in the center of the dough and fold in the circle so that it covers all of the butter.

4. Flour under and on top of the dough. Roll dough away and back toward you in the length and once in the width, without rolling over the ends, to make a rectangle about 15 inches long and 8 inches wide.

5. Fold the two 8-inch ends in toward the middle of the rectangle, leaving a 1-inch space in the middle. Fold the bottom up to the top to form 4 layers of dough. Place dough in the refrigerator for 20 minutes.

6. Repeat rolling and folding process (steps 4 and 5) two more times, refrigerating 20 minutes between each time. Wrap dough and refrigerate for 1 hour before using.

(continued on page 40)

(continued from page 38)

7. Preheat oven to 400°F.

8. After 1 hour, remove dough from refrigerator. Working on a lightly floured surface, roll the dough out into an ⅛-inch thick rectangle and place on a baking sheet lined with parchment paper. Use a fork to poke holes in the dough (as many as possible), line the dough with another sheet of parchment paper, and then place a second baking sheet on top (to act as a weight).

9. Bake for 25 minutes. Remove from oven and allow it to cool on a cooling rack for 2 hours before using.

10. Meanwhile, prepare the chocolate cream filling: Place the heavy cream and sugar in a small saucepan over medium heat and bring to a boil. When just boiling, remove from heat and add the chocolate and vanilla extract. Use a whisk to stir until all ingredients are combined.

11. Place chocolate cream in the freezer for 45 minutes before using. Once ready, transfer to a piping bag fitted with a round tip.

12. Place the prepared puff pastry sheets on a cutting board and use a sharp knife to cut three 4-inch by 6-inch rectangles. Place one rectangle on a large, flat serving plate and pipe the chocolate cream, about ½-inch high, onto the puff pastry. Place a second piece of puff pastry onto the chocolate cream and repeat the piping process. Top with the last piece of puff pastry and place in the freezer for 20 minutes.

13. After 20 minutes, remove the cake from the freezer. Use a sharp, serrated knife to cut the cake into 1-inch by 3-inch rectangles. Decorate each rectangle with cocoa powder and powdered sugar.

14. Cake can be stored in an airtight container in the freezer for up to 3 days.

Chocolate Mascarpone Cake

Serves

8

The Italian triple-cream cheese Mascarpone does wonders when added to a moist chocolate cake.

INGREDIENTS

For the cake

7 oz. unsweetened chocolate

1 stick (4 oz.) butter

1 cup all-purpose flour

½ teaspoon baking powder

6 eggs

⅔ cup sugar

For the mascarpone filling

1 cup mascarpone cheese

2 tablespoons cornstarch

¼ cup powdered sugar

For decoration

Powdered sugar

PREPARATION

1. Preheat oven to 350°F and butter a 12-cup fluted tube pan.

2. Melt chocolate and butter in a heatproof bowl, set over a pan of simmering water. Stir occasionally until chocolate has completely melted and the mixture is smooth. Remove from heat. Add the flour and baking powder, and stir until all ingredients are combined. Set aside to cool for 10 minutes.

3. Using a mixer fitted with a whisk attachment, mix the eggs and sugar together for about 7 minutes, until light and fluffy.

4. Using a rubber spatula, fold the egg mixture into the chocolate mixture until combined.

5. In a separate bowl, use a whisk to mix together the mascarpone, cornstarch and powdered sugar, until all the ingredients are combined and the mixture is smooth. Transfer mixture to a piping bag fitted with a ⅓-inch round tip.

6. Pour half of the batter into the prepared pan. Pipe the mascarpone mixture on top of the batter in a circular manner, starting from the center and working outwards until it reaches the edges of the pan. Pour the remaining batter on top of the mascarpone mixture.

7. Bake for 50 minutes. Allow cake to cool on a cooling rack for 1 hour.

8. Carefully release cake from pan and place on a serving plate. Decorate with powdered sugar and serve.

9. Cake may be stored in an airtight container at room temperature for up to 2 days.

Chocolate Mocha Cream Cake

Serves

6

Chocolate and coffee lovers, beware! This cake will become your new addiction.

INGREDIENTS

For the cake

8 oz. good quality unsweetened chocolate

2 sticks (8 oz.) butter

7 eggs

1 cup sugar

¾ cup all-purpose flour

2 tablespoons cocoa powder

For the mousse

4 oz. unsweetened chocolate

1 tablespoon (½ oz.) butter

1 tablespoon instant coffee (dissolved in 2 tablespoons boiling water)

2 cups heavy cream

½ cup powdered sugar

For decoration

Chocolate shavings

PREPARATION

1. Preheat oven to 350°F.

2. Melt chocolate and butter in a heatproof bowl, set over a pan of simmering water. Stir occasionally until chocolate has completely melted. Remove from heat.

3. Using a mixer fitted with a whisk attachment, whisk together the eggs and sugar on medium speed for about 7 minutes, until light and fluffy.

4. Using a rubber spatula, fold the flour and cocoa powder into the chocolate mixture until combined, and then fold the chocolate mixture into the egg mixture until all ingredients are incorporated.

5. Pour the mixture into a round 10-inch baking ring placed on a baking sheet lined with parchment paper. Bake for 20 minutes. Allow the cake to cool on a cooling rack for 40 minutes.

6. Prepare the mousse: Melt the chocolate and butter in a heatproof bowl, set over a pan of simmering water. Stir occasionally until chocolate has completely melted. Remove from heat. Add the instant coffee and mix until combined.

7. Using a mixer fitted with a whisk attachment, whisk together the heavy cream and powdered sugar on medium speed for 5 minutes until the whipped cream is firm.

(continued on page 44)

(continued from page 42)

8. Using a rubber spatula, fold the chocolate mixture into the whipped cream until the mixture is smooth.

9. Assemble the cake: Using a round 3-inch cookie cutter, cut six circles out of the prepared cake. Place 2 tablespoons of mousse on top of 3 cake circles. Top each cake circle with an additional cake circle.

10. Place another 2 tablespoons of mousse onto each cake circle and use an offset spatula to smooth out the top layer of mousse.

11. Place cakes onto a large serving plate and place in freezer for at least 2 hours, preferably overnight.

12. Remove cakes from freezer, decorate with chocolate shavings and serve.

13. Cake may be stored in the refrigerator for up to 3 days.

Baked Chocolate Tart

If you don't have a food processor, you can make this tart dough by hand. Just make sure that you are using very cold butter, and mix the ingredients together first with your hands. Then place it onto a work surface and knead until a ball of dough is formed.

INGREDIENTS

For the crust

1 stick (4 oz.) butter, very cold and cubed

2 tablespoons powdered sugar

1 egg

1 tablespoon, very cold water

$\frac{1}{2}$ teaspoon salt

$1\frac{1}{4}$ cups all-purpose flour

For the chocolate filling

2 cups unsweetened chocolate

$\frac{1}{2}$ stick (2 oz.) butter

1 tablespoon brandy

$\frac{1}{2}$ cup sugar

3 eggs

For decoration

1 tablespoon powdered sugar

PREPARATION

1. Make the crust: Place the butter and sugar in a food processor and mix for 2 minutes, wiping down the sides, until the mixture is smooth. Add the egg, water and salt, and continue mixing for another 2 minutes until all ingredients are combined. Add the flour and mix for another minute until dough is formed. Remove ball of dough, wrap in plastic wrap and refrigerate for at least 1 hour before using.

2. Preheat oven to 325°F.

3. Working on a lightly floured surface, roll out the dough to an $\frac{1}{8}$-inch thick. Carefully place the dough into an 11-inch tart pan. Using your fingers, stick the dough to the sides of the dish. Using a rolling pan, gently roll over the top of the pan to get rid of the remaining dough. Place the pan in the refrigerator for 15 minutes.

4. Meanwhile, make the filling: Melt chocolate and butter in a heatproof bowl, set over a pan of simmering water. Stir occasionally until chocolate has completely melted and the mixture is smooth. Remove from heat and add the brandy, sugar and eggs (one at a time), while constantly whisking, until all ingredients are combined and mixture is smooth.

5. Pour the chocolate filling evenly into the tart pan and bake for 45 minutes. Allow to cool on a cooling rack for 30 minutes. Decorate with powdered sugar and serve at room temperature.

6. Tart may be stored in the refrigerator for up to 2 days.

Death by Chocolate Cake

6

The term "death by chocolate" was coined in 1984 by a man named Erik Russell, who was working for a London-based dessert manufacturer at the time. Russell tasted a sample for a proposed new chocolate product and exclaimed, "This one's death by chocolate".

INGREDIENTS

For the cake

12 oz. good quality unsweetened chocolate

2 sticks (8 oz.) butter

7 eggs

1 cup sugar

1 cup all-purpose flour

2 tablespoons cocoa powder

For the chocolate cream filling

1 cup heavy cream

10 oz. unsweetened chocolate

For decoration

5 oz. unsweetened chocolate, broken into large pieces

PREPARATION

1. Preheat oven to 325°F and butter two round 8-inch springform pans.

2. Melt chocolate and butter in a heatproof bowl, set over a pan of simmering water. Stir occasionally until chocolate has melted completely. Remove from heat.

3. Using a mixer fitted with a whisk attachment, whisk together the eggs and sugar on medium speed for about 7 minutes, until light and fluffy.

4. Using a rubber spatula, fold the flour and cocoa powder into the chocolate mixture until combined, and then fold the chocolate mixture into the egg mixture until all ingredients are incorporated.

5. Pour the mixture evenly into the two prepared pans. Bake for 40 minutes. Allow the cakes to cool on a cooling rack for 1 hour.

6. Meanwhile, prepare the chocolate cream filling: Place the heavy cream in a small saucepan over medium heat and cook until just boiling. Remove from heat, add chocolate, and use a whisk to stir until chocolate is melted and the mixture is smooth.

7. Assemble the cake: Place one of the cakes on a large serving plate. Using an offset spatula, spread ⅓ of the cream filling onto the cake. Place cake in freezer for 15 minutes.

(continued on page 48)

(continued from page 46)

8. Remove cake from freezer and cover the cream filling with the second prepared cake. Place cake in freezer for 2 hours.

9. **Meanwhile, prepare the decoration:** Melt chocolate in a heatproof bowl, set over a pan of simmering water. Stir occasionally until chocolate has completely melted. Remove from heat.

10. Pour the chocolate onto a baking sheet lined with parchment paper. Use an offset spatula to smooth out the chocolate and create a very thin layer. Place baking sheet in the freezer for later use.

11. Remove cake from freezer and slightly reheat the chocolate cream filling (so that it can be spread easily). Use an offset spatula to cover the cake, top and sides, with the remaining chocolate cream.

12. Remove the chocolate decoration from the freezer and break the chocolate into large pieces. Stick the pieces of chocolate onto the cake.

13. Cake can be stored in the refrigerator for up to 3 days.

Chocolate Ricotta Cheese Cake

12

With a twist of ricotta and chocolate, this perfect cheesecake is rich and creamy. It's just the right dessert to follow a decadent meal.

INGREDIENTS

For the crust

1 cup graham cracker crumbs

½ cup ground almonds

1½ sticks (6 oz.) butter, melted

½ cup brown sugar

For the cake

6 oz. cream cheese

1½ cups sugar

15 oz. ricotta cheese

2 egg yolks + 2 eggs

1 teaspoon pure vanilla extract

2 tablespoons cocoa powder

½ teaspoon pure almond extract

For the frosting

⅓ cup heavy cream

4 oz. unsweetened chocolate

1 tablespoon (½ oz.) butter

PREPARATION

1. Preheat oven to 350°F and butter a round 10-inch springform pan.

2. Place all of the crust ingredients in a large bowl. Using a wooden spoon, mix until all ingredients are combined.

3. Turn the crust mixture into the prepared springform pan. Using your fingers, pat the mixture until an even layer covers the bottom of the pan. Place the pan in the freezer for later use.

4. Using a mixer fitted with a whisk attachment, mix the cream cheese and sugar on medium speed for 4 minutes, until smooth. Reduce mixer speed to low and gradually add the remaining cake ingredients. Once all the ingredients are added, mix for another 2 minutes until well combined.

5. Remove pan from freezer and pour the batter onto the crust. Bake for 1 hour. Make sure the center of the cake is fully baked before removing from oven. Allow cake to cool on cooling rack for 10 minutes, and then use a knife to separate the edges of the cake from the pan. Allow cake to cool on cooling rack for an additional hour.

6. **Prepare the frosting:** Place the heavy cream in a small saucepan and cook over medium heat until just boiling. Remove from heat and add the chocolate and butter. Using a whisk, mix until the chocolate has melted and the mixture is smooth. Allow to rest for 15 minutes before using.

7. Release the cake from the pan and place on a serving plate. Pour the frosting evenly over the cake, allowing it to drip down the sides. Place the cake in the freezer for 10 minutes before serving.

8. Cake may be stored in the refrigerator for up to 3 days.

Chocolate Poppy Seed Cake

Make sure to taste your poppy seeds before using them in the recipe. Poppy seeds have the tendency to go rancid quickly, which could really spoil this fabulous dessert!

INGREDIENTS

For the cake

10 oz. unsweetened chocolate

1½ sticks (6 oz.) butter

1 cup ground poppy seeds

½ teaspoon baking powder

6 eggs

½ cup sugar

For the frosting

⅓ cup heavy cream

5 oz. unsweetened chocolate

1 teaspoon brandy

PREPARATION

1. Preheat oven to 325°F and butter a round 9-inch springform pan.

2. Melt chocolate and butter in a large heatproof bowl, set over a pan of simmering water. Stir occasionally until chocolate has completely melted and the mixture is smooth. Remove from heat. Add the ground poppy seeds and baking powder, and stir until all ingredients are combined.

3. Using a mixer fitted with a whisk attachment, mix the eggs and sugar together for about 7 minutes, until light and fluffy.

4. Using a rubber spatula, fold the eggs into the chocolate mixture until combined.

5. Pour the batter evenly into the prepared pan and bake for 40 minutes. Allow to cool on a cooling rack for 1 hour.

6. Meanwhile, prepare the frosting: Place the heavy cream in a small saucepan and cook over medium heat until just boiling. Remove from heat and add the chocolate and brandy. Use a whisk to stir until all ingredients are combined. Allow to cool for 30 minutes before using.

7. Carefully remove cake from pan and place on a serving plate. Pour the frosting evenly over the cake, allowing it to drip down the sides. Place the cake in the freezer for 10 minutes before serving.

8. Cake can be stored in the refrigerator for up to 3 days.

Chocolate Prune Cake

Serves
10

This chocolate cake is perfect for the more health-conscious, as prunes contain a nutritious amount of dietary fiber.

INGREDIENTS

For the cake

9 oz. unsweetened chocolate

1½ sticks (6 oz.) butter

1 cup prunes, pitted and finely chopped

½ cup all-purpose flour

⅔ teaspoon baking powder

6 eggs

½ cup sugar

For the frosting

⅓ cup heavy cream

5 oz. unsweetened chocolate

1 teaspoon grappa

PREPARATION

1. Preheat oven to 325°F and butter a round 9-inch springform pan.

2. Melt chocolate and butter in a large heatproof bowl, set over a pan of simmering water. Stir occasionally until chocolate has completely melted and the mixture is smooth. Remove from heat. Add the chopped prunes, flour and baking powder, and stir until all ingredients are combined.

3. Using a mixer fitted with a whisk attachment, mix the eggs and sugar together for about 7 minutes, until light and fluffy.

4. Using a rubber spatula, fold the eggs into the chocolate mixture until combined.

5. Pour the batter evenly into the prepared pan and bake for 40 minutes. Allow to cool on a cooling rack for 1 hour.

6. Meanwhile, prepare the frosting: Place the heavy cream in a small saucepan and cook over medium heat until just boiling. Remove from heat and add the chocolate and grappa. Use a whisk to stir until all ingredients are combined. Allow to cool for 30 minutes before using.

7. Carefully remove cake from pan and place on a serving plate. Pour the frosting evenly over the cake, allowing it to drip down the sides. Place the cake in the freezer for 10 minutes before serving.

8. Cake can be stored in the refrigerator for up to 3 days.

Chocolate Brioche Cake

Serves

This cake is a bit time-consuming, but the aromas that will fill your house while this cake is baking are well worth the effort.

INGREDIENTS

For the dough

1 cup milk

1 large egg

2 tablespoons fresh yeast

3½ cups all-purpose flour

2 teaspoons salt

½ cup sugar

1 teaspoon lemon zest

2½ sticks (10 oz.) butter, very cold and cubed

For the chocolate filling

8 oz. unsweetened chocolate

5 oz. marzipan

2 sticks (8 oz.) butter

⅓ cup cocoa powder

1 teaspoon pure vanilla extract

½ cup powdered sugar

PREPARATION

1. Using a mixer fitted with a paddle attachment, mix together the milk, egg, yeast and flour on low speed for 3 minutes. Increase mixer speed to medium, add the salt, sugar, lemon zest and mix for 2 minutes, until all ingredients are incorporated.

2. Gradually add the cubes of butter while mixing for 6 minutes, at which point the dough should be very soft. Increase mixer speed to high and mix for 12-15 minutes, until the dough no longer sticks to the sides of the mixer.

3. Lightly flour the dough and transfer to a floured bowl, cover in plastic wrap and place in the refrigerator for at least 2 hours, preferably overnight.

4. Meanwhile, prepare the filling: Melt chocolate in a heatproof bowl, set over a pan of simmering water. Stir occasionally until chocolate has completely melted and the mixture is smooth.

5. Using a mixer fitted with paddle attachment, mix the marzipan and butter together on medium speed for 4 minutes, until ingredients are combined and mixture is smooth. Add the cocoa powder, powdered sugar, vanilla extract and melted chocolate, and continue mixing for another 2 minutes until all ingredients are incorporated.

6. Butter a 12-cup fluted tube pan.

7. Remove dough from refrigerator. Working on a lightly floured surface, roll out the dough to an ⅛-inch thick. Use an offset spatula to spread the filling onto the dough. Gently roll the dough lengthwise and secure the ends together, making a large ring.

8. Preheat oven to 350°F.

9. Place the dough into the prepared pan and allow the dough to rise in a dry, warm place for 1½ hours, until it has tripled in size.

10. Once the dough has risen, bake for 55-60 minutes, until dough is crisp and not soft. Allow to cool on a cooling rack for 1 hour before serving.

11. Cake may be stored in an airtight container at room temperature for up to 3 days.

Steamed Chocolate Cake

Serves

10

This recipe incorporates the method of steaming into the baking process, making the cakes perfectly moist and ready for serving. This cake also doesn't take to reheating well, so make it and serve immediately.

INGREDIENTS

8 oz. unsweetened chocolate

2 sticks (8 oz.) butter

1½ cups powdered sugar

6 eggs

⅔ cup flour

PREPARATION

1. Preheat oven to 325°F. Butter eight 3-inch baking rings (2 inches high).

2. Melt chocolate and butter in a heatproof bowl, set over a pan of simmering water. Stir occasionally until chocolate has completely melted and the mixture is smooth. Remove from heat, add powdered sugar and stir to combine.

3. Add the eggs (one at a time) and continue to stir until incorporated. Gradually add the flour and stir to combine.

4. Place the baking rings into a large, deep baking dish and pour the batter evenly into the each ring. Fill the dish with water, a ½-inch high, and cover dish with aluminum foil. Bake for 35 minutes.

5. Place cakes onto a serving plate, remove rings and serve immediately.

Chocolate Meringue Cake

Serves

12

Crispy meringue paired with creamy chocolate is what this cake is all about.

INGREDIENTS

For the cake

5 egg whites

2 cups sugar

2 tablespoons white wine vinegar

For the chocolate cream

¾ cup heavy cream

8 oz. unsweetened chocolate

3 egg whites

½ cup sugar

PREPARATION

1. Preheat oven to 300°F.

2. Using a mixer fitted with a whisk attachment, mix the egg whites on high speed for minutes until firm. Gradually add the sugar and continue to mix until combined. Gradually add the vinegar and continue to mix for another 2 minutes until glossy, white peaks are formed.

3. Place an 8-inch plate onto a baking sheet lined with parchment paper and draw an outline of the plate. Repeat until you have 5 circles drawn.

4. Place 2 tablespoons of the meringue onto each circle and use the back of a spoon to gently flatten out the meringue so that it fits the perimeter of the circle outline exactly. Bake for 1½ hours until the meringue is dry and crisp. Allow to cool on a cooling rack for 45 minutes.

5. Meanwhile, prepare the chocolate cream: Place the heavy cream in a small saucepan and cook over medium heat until just boiling. Remove from heat, add the chocolate, and use a whisk to stir until all ingredients are combined.

6. Using a mixer fitted with a whisk attachment, whisk the egg whites on high speed for 5 minutes until firm, and then gradually add the sugar and continue mixing for another 3 minutes, until all sugar is combined.

7. Using a rubber spatula, fold the egg whites into the chocolate mixture until combined.

8. Assemble the cake: Place 1 meringue piece onto a serving plate and spread 3 tablespoons of chocolate cream onto the meringue. Top with another piece of meringue and repeat process for the remaining 3 pieces of meringue.

9. Cake may be stored in the refrigerator for up to 2 days.

Hot Chocolate Cake

Serves

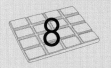

8

If you make the batter ahead of time, keep in mind that the baking time will be lengthened by 2-3 minutes. This is a cake that should be served right out of the oven, so I wouldn't recommend making in advance and reheating.

INGREDIENTS

8 oz. unsweetened chocolate

2 sticks (8 oz.) butter

1½ cups powdered sugar

4 eggs + 4 egg yolks

⅔ cup all-purpose flour

PREPARATION

1. Preheat oven to 350°F. Butter eight 3-inch baking rings (2 inches high).

2. Melt chocolate and butter in a heatproof bowl, set over a pan of simmering water. Stir occasionally until chocolate has completely melted and the mixture is smooth. Remove from heat, add powdered sugar and stir to combine.

3. Add the eggs (one at a time) and continue to stir until incorporated. Add the egg yolks (one at a time) and stir until mixture is smooth. Gradually add the flour and stir to combine. (This step can be done up to a few hours in advance and kept in the refrigerator).

4. Place the baking rings on a baking sheet lined with parchment paper. Pour the batter evenly into each ring. Bake for 10-12 minutes until the sides of the cake are cooked and the middle is soft to touch. Allow to cool for 2 minutes.

5. Place cakes onto a serving plate, remove rings and serve.

Molten Chocolate Cake

12

Famous chef Jean-Georges Vongerichten claims to have invented this now famous chocolate cake in New York City in 1987, but the French chef and chocolatier, Jacques Torres, has disputed his claim, arguing that the dessert already existed in France.

INGREDIENTS

For the cake

12 oz. unsweetened chocolate

2½ sticks (10 oz.) butter

1 tablespoon chocolate-flavored liqueur

6 eggs

1 cup sugar

For decoration

2 tablespoons cocoa powder

PREPARATION

1. Preheat oven to 350°F and butter a round 10-inch springform pan.

2. Melt chocolate and butter in a heatproof bowl, set over a pan of simmering water. Stir occasionally until chocolate has completely melted and the mixture is smooth. Remove from heat. Add the chocolate liqueur and stir until all ingredients are combined. Set aside to cool for 10 minutes.

3. Using a mixer fitted with a whisk attachment, mix the eggs and sugar together for about 7 minutes, until light and fluffy.

4. Using a rubber spatula, fold the eggs into the chocolate mixture until combined.

5. Pour the batter into the prepared pan, and then place the pan into a larger baking pan, filled with 2 cups of water. Bake for 30 minutes. Allow to cool on a cooling rack for 1 hour. Refrigerate for at least 8 hours, preferably overnight.

6. Carefully remove cake from pan and place on a serving plate. Decorate with cocoa powder and serve at room temperature.

7. Cake may be stored in the refrigerator for up to 3 days.

Double Chocolate Cake

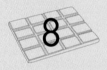

Serves

8

A cake for the true chocolate lovers among us; it's easy to make and even easier to devour.

INGREDIENTS

For the cake

10 oz. unsweetened chocolate

1½ sticks (6 oz.) butter

⅔ cup flour

½ teaspoon baking powder

6 eggs

½ cup sugar

1 cup chocolate chips

For the frosting

⅓ cup heavy cream

1 teaspoon instant coffee

5 oz. unsweetened chocolate

PREPARATION

1. Preheat oven to 325°F and butter a round 9-inch springform pan.

2. Melt chocolate and butter in a large heatproof bowl, set over a pan of simmering water. Stir occasionally until chocolate has completely melted and the mixture is smooth. Remove from heat. Add the flour and baking powder, and stir until all ingredients are combined. Set aside to cool for 10 minutes.

3. Using a mixer fitted with a whisk attachment, mix the eggs and sugar for about 7 minutes, until light and fluffy.

4. Using a rubber spatula, fold the eggs into the chocolate mixture until combined.

5. Pour half of the batter into the prepared pan and top with ½ cup of chocolate chips. Pour in the remaining batter and top with the remaining ½ cup of chocolate chips. Bake for 40 minutes. Allow to cool on a cooling rack for 1 hour.

6. Meanwhile, prepare the frosting: Place the heavy cream and coffee in a small saucepan and cook over medium heat until just boiling. Remove from heat and add the chocolate. Use a whisk to stir until all ingredients are combined. Allow to cool for 30 minutes before using.

7. Carefully remove cake from pan and place on a serving plate. Pour the frosting evenly over the cake, allowing it to drip down the sides. Place the cake in the freezer for 10 minutes before serving.

8. Cake can be stored in the refrigerator for up to 3 days.

Chocolate Almond Torte

Serves

10

This cake is the perfect combination of the all-time favorite pairing of almonds and chocolate.

INGREDIENTS

For the torte

10 oz. unsweetened chocolate

1¼ sticks (5 oz.) butter

¼ cup all-purpose flour

1 cup ground almonds

½ teaspoon baking powder

6 eggs

⅔ cup sugar

For the chocolate cream filling

⅓ cup heavy cream

5 oz. unsweetened chocolate

1 tablespoon almond-flavored liqueur, such as Amaretto

4 egg whites

½ cup sugar

For decoration

1 cup blanched almond slivers

PREPARATION

1. Preheat oven to 350°F and butter a round 9-inch springform pan.

2. Melt chocolate and butter in a heatproof bowl, set over a pan of simmering water. Stir occasionally until chocolate has completely melted and the mixture is smooth. Remove from heat. Add the flour, ground almonds and baking powder, and stir until all ingredients are combined. Set aside to cool for 10 minutes.

3. Using a mixer fitted with a whisk attachment, mix the eggs and sugar together for about 7 minutes, until light and fluffy.

4. Using a rubber spatula, fold the eggs into the chocolate mixture until combined.

5. Pour the batter into the prepared pan and bake for 40 minutes. Allow cake to cool on a cooling rack for 1 hour.

6. Meanwhile, prepare the cream filling: Place the heavy cream in a small saucepan and cook over medium heat until just boiling. Remove from heat and add the chocolate and almond liqueur. Use a whisk to stir until all ingredients are combined.

7. Using a mixer fitted with a whisk attachment, whisk the egg whites on high speed for 5 minutes until firm, and then gradually add the sugar and continue mixing for another 3 minutes, until all the sugar is combined.

8. Using a rubber spatula, fold the egg whites into the chocolate mixture until combined.

9. Assemble the cake: Carefully release the cake from the pan. Use a sharp, serrated knife to slice the cake in half, horizontally, so that after cutting you have two equal sheets of cake.

10. Place one layer onto a large serving plate and spread ⅓ of the cream filling onto the cake layer. Top with the second cake layer and place cake in the freezer for 15 minutes.

11. Remove cake from freezer and spread the remaining cream filling over the top and sides of cake. Decorate top and sides of cake with the almond slivers. Refrigerate for 1 hour before serving.

12. Cake may be stored in the refrigerator for up to 2 days.

Baked Chocolate Mousse Cake

Serves

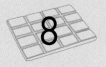

8

A perfect dessert to serve in the summer—the cold mousse gives a cool, refreshing feeling with every bite.

INGREDIENTS

For the cake

7 oz. unsweetened chocolate

1 stick (4 oz.) butter

¾ cup all-purpose flour

½ teaspoon baking powder

6 eggs

⅔ cup sugar

For the mousse

½ cup heavy cream

5 oz. unsweetened chocolate

1 teaspoon brandy

3 egg whites

½ cup sugar

For decoration

¼ cup cocoa powder

PREPARATION

1. Preheat oven to 350°F and butter a round 9-inch springform pan.

2. Melt chocolate and butter in a heatproof bowl, set over a pan of simmering water. Stir occasionally until chocolate has completely melted and the mixture is smooth. Remove from heat. Add the flour and baking powder, and stir until all ingredients are combined. Set aside to cool for 10 minutes.

3. Using a mixer fitted with a whisk attachment, mix the eggs and sugar together for about 7 minutes, until light and fluffy.

4. Using a rubber spatula, fold the eggs into the chocolate mixture until combined.

5. Pour batter into prepared pan and bake for 40 minutes. Allow cake to cool on cooling rack for 1 hour.

6. Meanwhile, prepare the mousse: Place the heavy cream in a small saucepan and cook over medium heat until just boiling. Remove from heat and add the chocolate and brandy. Use a whisk to stir until all ingredients are combined. Set aside to cool to room temperature.

7. Using a mixer fitted with a whisk attachment, whisk the egg whites on high speed for 5 minutes until firm. Gradually add the sugar and continue mixing for another 3 minutes, until all sugar is combined and glossy, white peaks form. Transfer to a large bowl.

(continued on page 64)

(continued from page 62)

8. Using a rubber spatula, fold the chocolate mixture into the egg whites until combined. Place the mousse in the freezer for 1 hour.

9. Assemble the cake: Remove mousse from freezer and using an ice cream scoop, scoop out mousse and place on the top of the cake. Repeat until the top of the cake is covered with scoops of mousse. This step should be done quickly. Decorate with cocoa powder and serve.

10. Cake may be stored in the refrigerator for up to 3 days.

Chocolate Charlotte Cake

Serves

8

Classically, this dessert was made by dipping stale bread into butter to use as the lining. This recipe calls for making your own lining, or you can use store-bought lady fingers just as well.

INGREDIENTS

For the dough

4 eggs, yolks and whites separated

⅔ cup sugar

½ cup all-purpose flour

2 tablespoons powdered sugar

For the cream filling

2 cups heavy cream

12 oz. unsweetened chocolate, cut into small cubes

1 pound fresh raspberries

PREPARATION

1. Preheat oven to 350°F.

2. Using a mixer fitted with a whisk attachment, whisk the egg whites on high speed for 5 minutes until firm. Gradually add half the sugar and continue mixing for another 4 minutes until glossy, white peaks form. Transfer to a clean bowl.

3. Place the egg yolks and the remaining sugar in the mixer fitted with a whisk attachment and whisk on high speed for 5 minutes, until light and fluffy. Pour the mixture into the bowl with egg whites and pour in the flour. Use a rubber spatula to carefully fold the mixture together, until all ingredients are combined. Transfer mixture to a piping bag fitted with a round tip.

4. Place a sheet of parchment paper onto a baking sheet and pipe two 10-inch circles onto the sheet. On a second baking sheet, lined with parchment paper, pipe 3-inch lines, close together, so that you have enough room for 2 rows, each row spaced 2 inches apart. Sprinkle powdered sugar on evenly.

5. Bake for 15 minutes. Allow to cool on a cooling rack for 30 minutes, until room temperature.

6. Meanwhile, prepare the cream filling: Place the heavy cream into a small saucepan over medium heat and cook until just boiling. Remove from heat and add chocolate. Use a whisk to stir until chocolate is melted and the mixture is smooth. Set aside for later use.

7. Assemble the cake: Place a 10-inch by 3-inch cake ring onto a baking sheet lined with parchment paper. Carefully remove one of the 10-inch baked cake circles from the parchment paper. Place the cake into the bottom of the cake ring. Carefully remove the cake lines from the parchment paper. Using the lines, create a border on top of the cake, along the sides of the ring.

8. Pour half of the cream filling into the ring and place half of the raspberries evenly on top of the filling. Place the cake in the freezer for 30 minutes.

9. Remove cake from the freezer and place the second cake circle on top of the raspberries. Pour in the remaining cream filling and top with the remaining raspberries. Place cake in the freezer for an additional 30 minutes. Allow cake to rest for 30 minutes before serving.

10. Cake may be stored in the refrigerator for up to 2 days.

Brownies

Fudgy Nut Brownies • Rich Brownies •

Pecan Brownies • Coconut Brownies •

Chocolate and Gianduja Brownies • Raisin-Filled Brownies •

Triple Chocolate Brownies • Ginger Cherry Brownies •

Apricot and Rum Brownies • Peanut Butter Brownies •

Mint Frosted Brownies • Prune and Red Wine Brownies •

Pear and Almond Brownies • White Chocolate Brownies •

Blondies • Cream Cheese Brownies •

Fudgy Nut Brownies

Makes

20

Nuts and brownies go together like peas and carrots.

INGREDIENTS

8 oz. good quality unsweetened chocolate

1½ sticks (6 oz.) butter

5 eggs

⅔ cup sugar

½ cup all-purpose flour

⅔ cup roasted hazelnuts, peeled

PREPARATION

1. Line an 8-inch by 10-inch baking pan with parchment paper. Preheat oven to 350°F.

2. Melt chocolate and butter in a heatproof bowl set over a pan of simmering water, stirring occasionally.

3. Using a mixer fitted with a whisk attachment, mix the eggs and sugar together for about 7 minutes, until soft and fluffy.

4. Using a flexible spatula, fold the flour into the chocolate and butter mixture until flour is combined. Fold the mixture into the whipped eggs until batter is smooth.

5. Pour batter evenly into the prepared baking pan and sprinkle the hazelnuts evenly on top. Bake for 15 minutes.

6. Remove from oven and cool on a wire rack for 30 minutes. Refrigerate for at least 2 hours after cooling. Cut into 2-inch squares. Serve at room temperature.

7. Brownies may be stored in an airtight container at room temperature for up to 3 days.

Rich Brownies

Makes
20

Everybody loves a good brownie, especially these rich, chocolaty ones.

INGREDIENTS

For the brownies

10 oz. good quality unsweetened chocolate

2 sticks (8 oz.) butter

5 eggs

¾ cup sugar

½ cup all-purpose flour

For the chocolate ganache (optional)

2 cups heavy cream

12 oz. unsweetened chocolate, cut into small cubes

PREPARATION

1. Line an 8-inch by 10-inch baking pan with parchment paper. Preheat oven to 330°F.

2. Melt chocolate and butter in a heatproof bowl set over a pan of simmering water, stirring occasionally.

3. Using a mixer fitted with a whisk attachment, mix the eggs and sugar together for about 7 minutes, until soft and fluffy.

4. Using a flexible spatula, fold the flour into the chocolate and butter mixture until flour is combined. Fold the mixture into the whipped eggs until batter is smooth.

5. Pour batter evenly into the prepared baking pan. Bake for 10 minutes.

6. Meanwhile, prepare the ganache: Place the heavy cream in a small saucepan over medium heat and cook until just boiling. Remove from heat and add chocolate. Use a whisk to stir until chocolate is melted and the mixture is smooth.

7. Remove brownies from oven and cool on a wire rack for 30 minutes. Refrigerate for at least 2 hours after cooling. Cut into 2-inch squares. Serve at room temperature, with the warm ganache.

8. Brownies may be stored in an airtight container at room temperature for up to 3 days.

Pecan Brownies

Makes

20

Pecans are a good source of protein and unsaturated fats. They also contain antioxidants, which have been known to reduce cholesterol.

INGREDIENTS

8 oz. good quality unsweetened chocolate

1½ sticks (6 oz.) butter

5 eggs

⅔ cup sugar

½ cup all-purpose flour

1 cup pecans

PREPARATION

1. Line an 8-inch by 10-inch baking pan with parchment paper. Preheat oven to 325°F.

2. Melt chocolate and butter in a heatproof bowl set over a pan of simmering water, stirring occasionally.

3. Using a mixer fitted with a whisk attachment, mix the eggs and sugar together for about 7 minutes, until soft and fluffy.

4. Using a flexible spatula, fold the flour into the chocolate and butter mixture until flour is combined. Fold the mixture into the whipped eggs until batter is smooth.

5. Pour batter evenly into the prepared baking pan and sprinkle the pecans evenly on top. Bake for 20 minutes.

6. Remove from oven and cool on a wire rack for 30 minutes. Refrigerate for at least 2 hours after cooling. Cut into 2-inch squares. Serve at room temperature.

7. Brownies may be stored in an airtight container at room temperature for up to 3 days.

Coconut Brownies

Makes

Coconut lovers will go mad for these chocolaty coconut brownies.

INGREDIENTS

8 oz. good quality unsweetened chocolate

1½ sticks (6 oz.) butter

5 eggs

⅔ cup sugar

¼ cup all-purpose flour

½ cup + 2 tablespoons shredded coconut

PREPARATION

1. Line an 8-inch by 10-inch baking pan with parchment paper. Preheat oven to 325°F.

2. Melt chocolate and butter in a heatproof bowl set over a pan of simmering water, stirring occasionally.

3. Using a mixer fitted with a whisk attachment, mix the eggs and sugar together for about 7 minutes, until soft and fluffy.

4. Using a flexible spatula, fold the flour and ½ cup shredded coconut into the chocolate and butter mixture until flour is combined. Fold the mixture into the whipped eggs until batter is smooth.

5. Pour batter evenly into the prepared baking pan and sprinkle the remaining 2 tablespoons of shredded coconut evenly on top. Bake for 18 minutes.

6. Remove from oven and cool on a wire rack for 30 minutes. Refrigerate for at least 2 hours after cooling. Cut into 2-inch squares. Serve at room temperature.

7. Brownies may be stored in an airtight container at room temperature for up to 3 days.

Chocolate and Gianduja Brownies

Makes

20

Invented in Italy, Gianduja is a sweet chocolate containing hazelnut paste, which can be found in specialty food shops.

INGREDIENTS

7 oz. good quality unsweetened chocolate

⅓ cup Gianduja paste

2 sticks (8 oz.) butter

5 eggs

¾ cup sugar

½ cup all-purpose flour

PREPARATION

1. Line an 8-inch by 10-inch baking pan with parchment paper. Preheat oven to 325°F.

2. Melt chocolate, Gianduja and butter in a heatproof bowl set over a pan of simmering water, stirring occasionally.

3. Using a mixer fitted with a whisk attachment, mix the eggs and sugar together for about 7 minutes, until soft and fluffy.

4. Using a flexible spatula, fold the flour into the chocolate and butter mixture until flour is combined. Fold the mixture into the whipped eggs until batter is smooth.

5. Pour batter evenly into the prepared baking pan. Bake for 18 minutes.

6. Remove from oven and cool on a wire rack for 30 minutes. Refrigerate for at least 2 hours after cooling. Cut into 2-inch squares. Serve at room temperature.

7. Brownies may be stored in an airtight container at room temperature for up to 3 days.

Raisin-Filled Brownies

Makes

Get your kids to love raisins by making these brownies for them.

INGREDIENTS

10 oz. good quality unsweetened chocolate

1½ sticks (6 oz.) butter

5 eggs

½ cup sugar

½ cup all-purpose flour

1 cup dark raisins

PREPARATION

1. Line an 8-inch by 10-inch baking pan with parchment paper. Preheat oven to 325°F.

2. Melt chocolate and butter in a heatproof bowl set over a pan of simmering water, stirring occasionally.

3. Using a mixer fitted with a whisk attachment, mix the eggs and sugar together for about 7 minutes, until soft and fluffy.

4. Using a flexible spatula, fold the flour into the chocolate and butter mixture until flour is combined. Fold the mixture into the whipped eggs until batter is smooth.

5. Spread the raisins evenly on the bottom of the prepared baking pan and pour batter evenly on top. Bake for 24 minutes.

6. Remove from oven and cool on a wire rack for 30 minutes. Refrigerate for at least 2 hours after cooling. Cut into 2-inch squares. Serve at room temperature.

7. Brownies may be stored in an airtight container at room temperature for up to 3 days.

Triple Chocolate Brownies

Makes

20

This recipe is for true chocolate lovers; the kind that don't discriminate between the types of chocolate.

INGREDIENTS

10 oz. good quality unsweetened chocolate

2 sticks (8 oz.) butter

5 eggs

¾ cup sugar

½ cup all-purpose flour

6 oz. milk chocolate, coarsely chopped

4 oz. white chocolate, coarsely chopped

PREPARATION

1. Line an 8-inch by 10-inch baking pan with parchment paper. Preheat oven to 325°F.

2. Melt unsweetened chocolate and butter in a heatproof bowl set over a pan of simmering water, stirring occasionally.

3. Using a mixer fitted with a whisk attachment, mix the eggs and sugar together for about 7 minutes, until soft and fluffy.

4. Using a flexible spatula, fold the flour into the chocolate mixture until flour is combined. Fold the mixture into the whipped eggs until batter is smooth.

5. Pour batter evenly into the prepared baking pan and sprinkle the milk chocolate and white chocolate evenly on top. Bake for 24 minutes.

6. Remove from oven and cool on a wire rack for 30 minutes. Refrigerate for at least 2 hours after cooling. Cut into 2-inch squares. Serve at room temperature.

7. Brownies may be stored in an airtight container at room temperature for up to 3 days.

Ginger Cherry Brownies

Makes

20

The candied ginger and cherry bites found in these brownies will provide a pleasant surprise with every bite.

INGREDIENTS

8 oz. good quality unsweetened chocolate

1½ sticks (6 oz.) butter

5 eggs

½ cup sugar

½ cup all-purpose flour

⅔ cup frozen cherries, pitted

⅓ cup candied ginger, finely chopped

PREPARATION

1. Line an 8-inch by 10-inch baking pan with parchment paper. Preheat oven to 325°F.

2. Melt chocolate and butter in a heatproof bowl set over a pan of simmering water, stirring occasionally.

3. Using a mixer fitted with a whisk attachment, mix the eggs and sugar together for about 7 minutes, until soft and fluffy.

4. Using a flexible spatula, fold the flour into the chocolate and butter mixture until flour is combined. Fold the mixture into the whipped eggs until batter is smooth.

5. Spread the cherries and candied ginger evenly on the bottom of the prepared baking pan, and pour batter evenly on top. Bake for 24 minutes.

6. Remove from oven and cool on a wire rack for 30 minutes. Refrigerate for at least 2 hours after cooling. Cut into 2-inch squares. Serve at room temperature.

7. Brownies may be stored in an airtight container at room temperature for up to 3 days.

Apricot and Rum Brownies

Makes **20**

These brownies are the perfect treat for the adult crowd.

INGREDIENTS

1 cup dried apricots

¼ cup dark rum

10 oz. good quality unsweetened chocolate

2 sticks (8 oz.) butter

5 eggs

½ cup sugar

½ cup all-purpose flour

PREPARATION

1. Place the dried apricots and rum in a medium bowl and allow the apricots to soak for 1 hour.

2. Line an 8-inch by 10-inch baking pan with parchment paper. Preheat oven to 325°F.

3. Melt chocolate and butter in a heatproof bowl set over a pan of simmering water, stirring occasionally.

4. Using a mixer fitted with a whisk attachment, mix the eggs and sugar together for about 7 minutes, until soft and fluffy.

5. Using a flexible spatula, fold the flour into the chocolate and butter mixture until flour is combined. Fold the mixture into the whipped eggs until batter is smooth.

6. Strain the apricots from the rum, reserving the rum. Spread the apricots evenly on the bottom of the prepared baking pan. Stir the remaining rum into the batter and pour batter evenly on top. Bake for 24 minutes.

7. Remove from oven and cool on a wire rack for 30 minutes. Refrigerate for at least 2 hours after cooling. Cut into 2-inch squares. Serve at room temperature.

8. Brownies may be stored in an airtight container at room temperature for up to 3 days.

Peanut Butter Brownies

Makes

I made these with smooth peanut butter, but you can substitute it with the chunky version if that's your preference.

INGREDIENTS

6 oz. good quality unsweetened chocolate

½ cup smooth peanut butter

1 stick (4 oz.) butter

5 eggs

½ cup sugar

½ cup all-purpose flour

PREPARATION

1. Line an 8-inch by 10-inch baking pan with parchment paper. Preheat oven to 325°F.

2. Melt chocolate, peanut butter and butter in a heatproof bowl set over a pan of simmering water, stirring occasionally.

3. Using a mixer fitted with a whisk attachment, mix the eggs and sugar together for about 7 minutes, until soft and fluffy.

4. Using a flexible spatula, fold the flour into the chocolate mixture until flour is combined. Fold the mixture into the whipped eggs until batter is smooth.

5. Pour batter evenly into the prepared baking pan. Bake for 24 minutes.

6. Remove from oven and cool on a wire rack for 30 minutes. Refrigerate for at least 2 hours after cooling. Cut into 2-inch squares. Serve at room temperature.

7. Brownies may be stored in an airtight container at room temperature for up to 3 days.

Mint Frosted Brownies

Makes

20

The fresh mint frosting gives these brownies a very refreshing twist.

INGREDIENTS

7 oz. good quality unsweetened chocolate

1¼ sticks (5 oz.) butter

5 eggs

¾ cup sugar

½ cup all-purpose flour

For the frosting

2 tablespoons fresh mint leaves

¼ stick (1 oz.) butter, softened

1 tablespoon whole milk

2 tablespoons cream cheese

2 cups powdered sugar

PREPARATION

1. Line an 8-inch by 10-inch baking pan with parchment paper. Preheat oven to 350°F.

2. Melt chocolate and butter in a heatproof bowl set over a pan of simmering water, stirring occasionally.

3. Using a mixer fitted with a whisk attachment, mix the eggs and sugar together for about 7 minutes, until soft and fluffy.

4. Using a flexible spatula, fold the flour into the chocolate and butter mixture until flour is combined. Fold the mixture into the whipped eggs until batter is smooth.

5. Pour batter evenly into the prepared baking pan. Bake for 15 minutes.

6. Meanwhile, prepare the frosting: Place the mint leaves, butter and milk in a food processor and blend until the mixture is smooth. Add the cream cheese and powdered sugar and continue mixing until a smooth, creamy, light green frosting is formed.

7. Remove brownies from oven and cool on a wire rack for 30 minutes. Using an offset spatula or the back of a knife, spread the frosting evenly onto the brownies. Refrigerate for at least 2 hours after frosting. Cut into 2-inch squares. Serve at room temperature.

8. Brownies may be stored in an airtight container at room temperature for up to 3 days.

Prune and Red Wine Brownies

20

When using wine for cooking, you don't have to go overboard with expensive wine. Just make sure that it is wine that would be suitable for drinking.

INGREDIENTS

1 cup prunes

¾ cup dry red wine

10 oz. good quality unsweetened chocolate

2 sticks (8 oz.) butter

5 eggs

½ cup sugar

½ cup all-purpose flour

PREPARATION

1. Place the prunes and red wine in a small saucepan over medium-high heat and bring to a boil. When boiling, reduce heat to low and cook for 20 minutes. Remove from heat and strain prunes, reserving the wine. Keep the prunes in refrigerator for later use.

2. Line an 8-inch by 10-inch baking pan with parchment paper. Preheat oven to 325°F.

3. Melt chocolate and butter in a heatproof bowl set over a pan of simmering water, stirring occasionally.

4. Using a mixer fitted with a whisk attachment, mix the eggs and sugar together for about 7 minutes, until soft and fluffy.

5. Using a flexible spatula, fold the flour into the chocolate and butter mixture until flour is combined. Add the remaining wine and stir to combine. Fold the mixture into the whipped eggs until batter is smooth.

6. Spread the prunes evenly on the bottom of the prepared baking pan and pour batter evenly on top. Bake for 24 minutes.

7. Remove from oven and cool on a wire rack for 30 minutes. Refrigerate for at least 2 hours after cooling. Cut into 2-inch squares. Serve at room temperature.

8. Brownies may be stored in an airtight container at room temperature for up to 3 days.

Pear and Almond Brownies

Makes

Make sure to use ripe pears for this recipe; the juiciness of the pears contributes to one of the moistest brownies around.

INGREDIENTS

8 oz. good quality unsweetened chocolate

1½ sticks (6 oz.) butter

5 eggs

¾ cup sugar

½ cup all-purpose flour

5 ripe pears, peeled and quartered

½ cup blanched almond slivers

PREPARATION

1. Line an 8-inch by 10-inch baking pan with parchment paper. Preheat oven to 325°F.

2. Melt chocolate and butter in a heatproof bowl set over a pan of simmering water, stirring occasionally.

3. Using a mixer fitted with a whisk attachment, mix the eggs and sugar together for about 7 minutes, until soft and fluffy.

4. Using a flexible spatula, fold the flour into the chocolate and butter mixture until flour is combined. Fold the mixture into the whipped eggs until batter is smooth.

5. Pour batter evenly into the prepared baking pan and place the pear quarters into the batter, spacing them uniformly. Sprinkle the almond slivers on top of the pears. Bake for 22 minutes.

6. Remove from oven and cool on a wire rack for 30 minutes. Refrigerate for at least 2 hours after cooling. Cut into 2-inch squares. Serve at room temperature.

7. Brownies may be stored in an airtight container at room temperature for up to 3 days.

White Chocolate Brownies

Makes

20

These brownies are actually not brown at all; white chocolate lovers can finally enjoy a brownie made only from white chocolate.

INGREDIENTS

8 oz. good quality white chocolate

1½ sticks (6 oz.) butter

5 eggs

⅔ cup sugar

½ cup all-purpose flour

⅔ cup white chocolate, coarsely chopped

PREPARATION

1. Line an 8-inch by 10-inch baking pan with parchment paper. Preheat oven to 350°F.

2. Melt 8 oz. white chocolate and butter in a heatproof bowl set over a pan of simmering water, stirring occasionally.

3. Using a mixer fitted with a whisk attachment, mix the eggs and sugar together for about 7 minutes, until soft and fluffy.

4. Using a flexible spatula, fold the flour into the chocolate and butter mixture until flour is combined. Fold the mixture into the whipped eggs until batter is smooth.

5. Pour batter evenly into the prepared baking pan and sprinkle the chopped white chocolate on top. Bake for 22 minutes.

6. Remove from oven and cool on a wire rack for 30 minutes. Refrigerate for at least 2 hours after cooling. Cut into 2-inch squares. Serve at room temperature.

7. Brownies may be stored in an airtight container at room temperature for up to 3 days.

Blondies

Makes

24

Blondies, the cousin of the brownie, are brown sugar-based dessert bars that closely resemble their chocolate counterpart.

INGREDIENTS

2 sticks (8 oz.) butter

1½ cups brown sugar

2 eggs

1 teaspoon pure vanilla extract

½ teaspoon baking powder

¼ teaspoon baking soda

2 cups all-purpose flour

½ cup chocolate chips

PREPARATION

1. Line an 8-inch by 12-inch baking pan with parchment paper. Preheat oven to 350°F.

2. Using a mixer fitted with a whisk attachment, mix together the butter and brown sugar on medium speed for 3 minutes, until the mixture is smooth. Add the eggs and vanilla extract and mix for another minute.

3. Gradually add the baking powder, baking soda and flour to the mixer, and continue to mix for another 2 minutes until all ingredients are combined. Turn off mixer.

4. Using a wooden spoon or flexible spatula, stir in the chocolate chips.

5. Pour batter evenly into the prepared baking pan and bake for 22 minutes.

6. Remove from oven and cool on a wire rack for 45 minutes. Cut into 2-inch squares.

7. Blondies may be stored in an airtight container at room temperature for up to 3 days.

Cream Cheese Brownies

Makes

20

Munching on these brownies is like eating a bite-sized chocolate cheesecake.

INGREDIENTS

7 oz. good quality unsweetened chocolate

2 sticks (8 oz.) butter

5 eggs

¾ cup sugar

½ cup all-purpose flour

⅓ cup cream cheese

⅓ cup powdered sugar

PREPARATION

1. Line an 8-inch by 10-inch baking pan with parchment paper. Preheat oven to 325°F.

2. Melt chocolate and butter in a heatproof bowl set over a pan of simmering water, stirring occasionally.

3. Using a mixer fitted with a whisk attachment, mix the eggs and sugar together for about 7 minutes, until soft and fluffy.

4. Using a flexible spatula, fold the flour into the chocolate and butter mixture until flour is combined. Fold the mixture into the whipped eggs until batter is smooth.

5. Pour batter evenly into the prepared baking pan.

6. In a separate bowl, mix together the cream cheese and powdered sugar until mixture is combined and has a creamy texture. Using a large spoon, spoon the cream cheese mixture onto the batter, 1 spoonful at a time, spacing 1 inch apart.

7. Using a toothpick, swirl in the cream cheese mixture into the batter to create a marble. Bake for 28-30 minutes.

8. Remove from oven and cool on a wire rack for 30 minutes. Refrigerate for at least 2hours after cooling. Cut into 2-inch squares. Serve at room temperature.

9. Browniers may be stored in an airtight container at room temperature for up to 3 days.

Bars

Turtle Bars • Hello Dolly Bars •

Chocolate Raisin and Nut Bars • Chocolate Chip Bars •

Chocolate Candy Bars • Coconut Chocolate Bars •

Chocolate Caramel Bars • Chocolate and Dried Fruit Treats •

Trail Mix Bars • Chocolate and Hazelnut Bars •

Chocolate Nougat Bites • Chocolate-Covered Marshmallow Bars •

Chocolate Marzipan Squares • Cornflake Bars •

Granola Bars • Crispy Chocolate Chip Squares •

Chocolate Blondie Squares • Crunch Bars •

Crispy Chocolate and Hazelnut Treats • Chocolate Date Bars •

Chocolate and Almond Crispy Treat • Triple Chocolate Bites •

Chocolate Sable Bars • Crispy Chocolate and Almond Fingers •

Chocolate Whisky Squares •

Turtle Bars

Makes

40

These caramel chocolate bars are a great snack to have around the house, but also work as a bite-sized dessert for any meal.

INGREDIENTS

For the caramel

⅔ cup sugar

½ cup heavy cream

For the chocolate

½ cup heavy cream

10 oz. unsweetened chocolate

½ cup hazelnuts, chopped

PREPARATION

1. Line the bottom of an 8-inch by 5-inch baking pan with parchment paper (cutting it to fit the bottom of the pan exactly). Preheat oven to 350°F.

2. **Prepare the caramel:** Heat the sugar in a small saucepan over medium heat until the sugar melts completely and has turned into a dark brown caramel. Lower the heat, add ⅓ cup of heavy cream, and gently stir with a wooden spoon until mixture is combined. Once mixture has thickened, add the remaining heavy cream and stir continuously until the mixture for about 6-8 minutes, until it has thickened significantly.

3. Pour the caramel into the prepared baking dish in an even layer and immediately place in freezer.

4. **Meanwhile, prepare the chocolate:** Heat the heavy cream in a medium saucepan over medium heat until just boiling, and then remove from heat. Using a whisk, stir in the chocolate until mixture is combined and smooth.

5. Remove baking pan with caramel from freezer and spread the chopped hazelnuts evenly over the caramel. Pour the chocolate mixture evenly over the hazelnuts. Place the baking pan in the freezer for at least 2 hours, preferably overnight.

6. Remove baking pan from freezer and flip the pan over. Gently peel off the parchment paper and cut bars into 1-inch squares.

7. Bars can be stored in an airtight container in the refrigerator for up to 3 days.

Hello Dolly Bars

24

These bars, also known as seven layer bars, are a mixture of all the perfect snack ingredients.

INGREDIENTS

1 stick (4 oz.) butter

1 cup graham cracker crumbs

1 cup shredded coconut

1 cup hazelnuts, chopped

1 cup chocolate chips

15 oz. sweet condensed milk

PREPARATION

1. Line an 8-inch by 12-inch baking pan with parchment paper. Preheat oven to 350°F.

2. Heat the butter in a small saucepan over low heat until the butter has melted. Remove from heat and stir in the graham cracker crumbs, until crumbs are fully coated with butter. Place the mixture into the prepared baking pan, spreading it out evenly to create a uniform layer.

3. Spread the coconut evenly over the graham crackers in a single layer. Continue making an even layer with the chopped hazelnuts, and then an additional layer with the chocolate chips.

4. Pour the condensed milk evenly over the baking pan, creating an even top layer. Do not mix the layers at any point during the preparation.

5. Bake for 28 minutes. Remove from oven and cool on a wire rack for 1 hour. Once cooled, refrigerate for 1 hour. Remove from refrigerator and cut into 2-inch squares immediately.

6. Bars can be stored in an airtight container at room temperature for up to 3 days.

Chocolate Raisin and Nut Bars

Makes

40

These bars are the perfect mix of healthy snack and chocolaty treat.

INGREDIENTS

½ cup heavy cream

10 oz. unsweetened chocolate

½ cup dark raisins

½ cup walnuts, halved

PREPARATION

1. Line the bottom of an 8-inch by 5-inch baking pan with parchment paper (cutting it to fit the bottom of the pan exactly). Preheat oven to 350°F.

2. Heat the heavy cream in a medium saucepan over medium heat until just boiling, and then remove from heat. Using a whisk, stir in the chocolate until mixture is combined and smooth. Add the raisins and walnuts, and mix until all ingredients are incorporated.

3. Pour the mixture into the prepared baking pan and place in the freezer for at least 2 hours, preferably overnight.

4. Remove baking pan from freezer and flip the pan over. Gently peel off the parchment paper and cut bars into 1-inch squares.

5. Bars can be stored in an airtight container in the refrigerator for up to 5 days.

Chocolate Chip Bars

Makes

40

Super easy to make, these bars are a guaranteed favorite with even the pickiest kid.

INGREDIENTS

½ cup heavy cream

10 oz. unsweetened chocolate

½ cup white chocolate chips

½ cup unsweetened chocolate chips

PREPARATION

1. Line the bottom of an 8-inch by 5-inch baking pan with parchment paper (cutting it to fit the bottom of the pan exactly). Preheat oven to 350°F.

2. Heat the heavy cream in a medium saucepan over medium heat until just boiling, and then remove from heat. Using a whisk, stir in the chocolate until mixture is combined and smooth.

3. Pour half of the chocolate mixture into the prepared baking pan and place in freezer for 10 minutes.

4. Remove from freezer and evenly sprinkle a ¼ cup of the white chocolate chips and a ¼ cup of the unsweetened chocolate chips on top of the chocolate that has been in the freezer. Pour the remaining chocolate mixture over the chocolate chips and then sprinkle on the remaining white chocolate chips and unsweetened chocolate chips. Place the baking pan in the freezer for at least 2 hours, preferably overnight.

5. Remove baking pan from freezer and flip the pan over. Gently peel off the parchment paper and cut bars into 1-inch squares.

6. Bars can be stored in an airtight container in the refrigerator for up to 5 days.

Chocolate Candy Bars

Makes

16

You can pretty much use any candy of your choice here. I prefer M&Ms because they are easy to find and add color to this chocolate dish.

INGREDIENTS

½ cup heavy cream

10 oz. unsweetened chocolate

1 cup colored sprinkles

1 cup candy-coated chocolate, such as M&Ms®

PREPARATION

1. Line the bottom of an 8-inch by 5-inch baking pan with parchment paper (cutting it to fit the bottom of the pan exactly). Preheat oven to 350°F.

2. Heat the heavy cream in a medium saucepan over medium heat until just boiling, and then remove from heat. Using a whisk, stir in the chocolate until mixture is combined and smooth.

3. Pour the chocolate mixture evenly into the prepared baking pan and place in freezer for 10 minutes.

4. Remove from freezer and sprinkle the colored sprinkles evenly over the chocolate mixture and then decorate with the candy coated chocolates. Place the baking pan in the freezer for at least 2 hours, preferably overnight.

5. Remove baking pan from freezer and flip the pan over. Gently peel off the parchment paper and cut bars into 4-inch by 1-inch rectangles.

6. Bars can be stored in an airtight container in the refrigerator for up to 5 days.

Coconut Chocolate Bars

Makes

16

The perfect bar for a more sophisticated palate.

INGREDIENTS

½ cup heavy cream

10 oz. unsweetened chocolate

1 tablespoon coconut liqueur or coconut-flavored rum

½ cup shredded coconut

PREPARATION

1. Line the bottom of an 8-inch by 5-inch baking pan with parchment paper (cutting it to fit the bottom of the pan exactly). Preheat oven to 350°F.

2. Heat the heavy cream in a medium saucepan over medium heat until just boiling, and then remove from heat. Using a whisk, stir in the chocolate until mixture is combined and smooth. Add the coconut liqueur and mix until incorporated.

3. Pour half of the chocolate mixture into the prepared baking pan and evenly sprinkle a ¼ cup of the ground coconut on top of the chocolate. Place in freezer for 10 minutes.

4. Remove from freezer and pour on the remaining chocolate mixture. Sprinkle the remaining ground coconut evenly over the chocolate. Place the baking pan in the freezer for at least 2 hours, preferably overnight.

5. Remove baking pan from freezer and flip the pan over. Gently peel off the parchment paper and cut bars into 3-inch by 1-inch rectangles.

6. Bars can be stored in an airtight container in the refrigerator for up to 5 days.

Chocolate Caramel Bars

40

One layer of caramel plus one layer of pecans plus one layer of chocolate equals this delicious, easy-to-make recipe.

INGREDIENTS

For the caramel

½ cup sugar

⅓ cup heavy cream

½ cup pecans, finely chopped

For the chocolate

½ cup heavy cream

10 oz. unsweetened chocolate

PREPARATION

1. Line the bottom of an 8-inch by 5-inch baking pan with parchment paper (cutting it to fit the bottom of the pan exactly). Preheat oven to 350°F.

2. **Prepare the caramel:** Heat the sugar in a small saucepan over medium heat until the sugar melts completely and has turned into a dark brown caramel. Lower the heat, add the heavy cream, and stir continuously for about 6-8 minutes, until the mixture has thickened significantly.

3. Pour the caramel into the prepared baking dish in an even layer and place in the freezer for 10 minutes. After 10 minutes, remove from freezer and sprinkle the chopped pecans evenly on top of the caramel. Return baking dish to freezer.

4. **Meanwhile, prepare the chocolate:** Heat the heavy cream in a medium saucepan over medium heat until just boiling, and then remove from heat. Using a whisk, stir in the chocolate until mixture is combined and smooth.

5. Remove baking pan from freezer and pour the chocolate mixture evenly onto the caramel. Place the baking pan in the freezer for at least 2 hours, preferably overnight.

6. Remove baking pan from freezer and flip the pan over. Gently peel off the parchment paper and cut bars into 1-inch squares.

7. Bars can be stored in an airtight container in the refrigerator for up to 3 days.

Chocolate and Dried Fruit Treats

Makes

15

I used dried cranberries and dried apricots for this recipe, but you can substitute with the same amount of any dried fruit you have available in your pantry.

INGREDIENTS

½ cup heavy cream

10 oz. unsweetened chocolate

¼ cup dark raisins

½ cup walnuts, halved

½ cup dried cranberries

¼ cup dried apricots, finely chopped

¼ cup sesame seeds

PREPARATION

1. Line the bottom of a 9-inch by 5-inch baking pan with parchment paper (cutting it to fit the bottom of the pan exactly).

2. Heat the heavy cream in a medium saucepan over medium heat until just boiling, and then remove from heat. Using a whisk, stir in the chocolate until mixture is combined and smooth. Add all remaining ingredients and stir to combine.

3. Pour the chocolate mixture into the prepared baking pan and place in freezer for at least 2 hours, preferably overnight.

4. Remove baking pan from freezer and flip the pan over. Gently peel off the parchment paper and cut into 3-inch by 1-inch rectangles.

5. Bars can be stored in an airtight container in the refrigerator for up to 5 days.

Trail Mix Bars

Makes

40

These bars are like eating a bag of trail mix, combined with the perfect amount of chocolate.

INGREDIENTS

½ cup heavy cream

10 oz. unsweetened chocolate

¼ cup dark raisins

¼ cup walnuts, halved

¼ cup dried cranberries

¼ cup blanched almonds, halved

PREPARATION

1. Line the bottom of an 8-inch by 5-inch baking pan with parchment paper (cutting it to fit the bottom of the pan exactly). Preheat oven to 350°F.

2. Heat the heavy cream in a medium saucepan over medium heat until just boiling, and then remove from heat. Using a whisk, stir in the chocolate until mixture is combined and smooth.

3. Pour the chocolate mixture into the prepared baking pan and place in freezer for 10 minutes. Meanwhile, in a large bowl, combine all remaining ingredients.

4. After 10 minutes, remove from freezer and sprinkle the dry ingredients evenly over the chocolate. Return the baking pan to the freezer for at least 2 hours, preferably overnight.

5. Remove baking pan from freezer and flip the pan over. Gently peel off the parchment paper and cut bars into 1-inch squares.

6. Bars can be stored in an airtight container in the refrigerator for up to 5 days.

Chocolate and Hazelnut Bars

Makes

40

Hazelnuts are rich in protein and contain significant amounts of thiamine and vitamin B6—all the more reason to make these delicious treats.

INGREDIENTS

½ cup heavy cream

10 oz. unsweetened chocolate

1 tablespoon almond-flavored liqueur, such as Amaretto

1½ cups hazelnuts, coarsely chopped

PREPARATION

1. Line the bottom of an 8-inch by 5-inch baking pan with parchment paper (cutting it to fit the bottom of the pan exactly). Preheat oven to 350°F.

2. Heat the heavy cream in a medium saucepan over medium heat until just boiling, and then remove from heat. Using a whisk, stir in the chocolate until mixture is combined and smooth. Add the almond liqueur and mix until incorporated.

3. Pour the chocolate mixture into the prepared baking pan and place in freezer for 10 minutes. After 10 minutes, remove from freezer and sprinkle the chopped hazelnuts evenly over the chocolate. Return the baking pan to the freezer for at least 2 hours, preferably overnight.

4. Remove baking pan from freezer and flip the pan over. Gently peel off the parchment paper and cut bars into 1-inch squares.

5. Bars can be stored in an airtight container in the refrigerator for up to 5 days.

Chocolate Nougat Bites

Makes

40

Nougat is a nut-based paste which can be found in specialty baking shops, where you can also buy candied chopped hazelnuts.

INGREDIENTS

For the nougat crust

½ cup roasted hazelnuts, finely chopped

¾ cup nougat paste

1 teaspoon almond-flavored liqueur, such as Amaretto

4 oz. unsweetened chocolate, melted

For the topping

½ cup heavy cream

10 oz. unsweetened chocolate

1 tablespoon almond-flavored liqueur, such as Amaretto

¾ cup candied chopped hazelnuts, store-bought

PREPARATION

1. Line the bottom of an 8-inch by 5-inch baking pan with parchment paper (cutting it to fit the bottom of the pan exactly).

2. Make the nougat crust: In a small bowl, mix together the chopped hazelnuts, nougat paste and almond liqueur. Add the melted chocolate, stir until combined and then pour the mixture evenly into the prepared baking pan. Place baking pan in freezer.

3. Make the topping: Heat the heavy cream in a medium saucepan over medium heat until just boiling, and then remove from heat. Using a whisk, stir in the chocolate until mixture is combined and smooth. Add the almond liqueur and mix until incorporated.

4. Remove baking pan from freezer and pour chocolate mixture over nougat crust. Return to freezer for an additional 10 minutes.

5. Remove baking pan from freezer and sprinkle the candied hazelnuts evenly over the chocolate layer. Return to freezer for at least 2 hours, preferably overnight.

6. Remove baking pan from freezer and flip the pan over. Gently peel off the parchment paper and cut bars into 1-inch squares.

7. Bars can be stored in an airtight container in the refrigerator for up to 5 days.

Chocolate-Covered Meringue Bars

Makes

12

This is probably one of the more difficult recipes in the book. Make sure to read through all the steps before starting, and that everything is clear before getting down to work. Once you make this recipe and get the hang of it, it will be hard to go back to eating the store-bought kind.

INGREDIENTS

For the nougat crust

¾ cup nougat paste

½ cup roasted hazelnuts, finely chopped

¾ cup breakfast cereal, such as cornflakes, crumbled

5 oz. unsweetened chocolate, melted

For the meringue

⅔ cup sugar

2 tablespoons water

3 egg whites

For the chocolate shell

5 oz. unsweetened chocolate

1 tablespoon canola oil

PREPARATION

1. Line the bottom of an 8-inch by 5-inch baking pan with parchment paper (cutting it to fit the bottom of the pan exactly).

2. Make the nougat crust: In a small bowl, mix together the nougat paste, chopped hazelnuts and cereal. Add the melted chocolate, stir until combined and then pour the mixture evenly into the prepared baking pan. Place baking pan in freezer for 1 hour.

3. Remove baking pan from freezer and flip the pan over. Gently peel off the parchment paper and cut the cookies into 4-inch by 1½-inch rectangles. Place the cookie rectangles onto a large flat plate and place in the freezer.

4. Prepare the meringue: Place the sugar and water in a small saucepan over medium heat and bring to a boil. Meanwhile, using a stand mixer fitted with a whisk attachment, whip the egg whites at medium speed until glossy white peaks form.

5. Once the water reaches a boil, continue cooking for 3 minutes and then use a baking thermometer to check the temperature (it should be 250°F). Once the mixture reaches 250°F, remove from heat and gradually pour the mixture into the mixer bowl with the egg whites, while whisking at medium speed.

(continued on page 118)

(continued from page 116)

6. Increase mixer speed to high and whisk for 20 minutes, until mixture has cooled. Check by touching the sides of the mixer bowl, which should be cool to touch. If they aren't, continue mixing for another 5 minutes.

7. Transfer the mixture into a piping bag fitted with a ⅓-inch tip. Remove cookie rectangles from the freezer and pipe the meringue onto each cookie in a circular fashion so that the meringue in the middle of the cookie is higher. Return to freezer and prepare the chocolate shell.

8. Melt chocolate and oil in a heatproof bowl set over a pan of simmering water, stirring occasionally until the chocolate is melted and the mixture is smooth.

9. Working relatively fast, remove meringue cookies from freezer, place them on a cooling rack set over a tray or large plate. Carefully dip each meringue cookie into the melted chocolate so that the chocolate fully covers the cookie. Repeat with each of the bars. Place bars in the freezer for 20 minutes and then serve.

10. Bars can be stored in an airtight container in the refrigerator for up to 2 days.

Chocolate Marzipan Squares

40

Marzipan is a popular confection consisting primarily of sugar and almond meal. It can be found at specialty food shops or even at your local supermarket.

INGREDIENTS

½ cup heavy cream

10 oz. unsweetened chocolate

1 tablespoon almond-flavored liqueur, such as Amaretto

8 oz. good quality almond-based marzipan

PREPARATION

1. Line the bottom of an 8-inch by 5-inch baking pan with parchment paper (cutting it to fit the bottom of the pan exactly).

2. Heat the heavy cream in a medium saucepan over medium heat until just boiling, and then remove from heat. Using a whisk, stir in the chocolate until mixture is combined and smooth. Add the liqueur and stir to combine.

3. Pour half of the chocolate mixture into the prepared baking pan and place in freezer for 10 minutes.

4. Meanwhile, cover the marzipan with plastic wrap and use a rolling pin to roll it into an 8-inch by 5-inch rectangle.

5. After 10 minutes, remove the baking pan from the freezer and carefully place the rolled-out marzipan over the chocolate mixture. Pour the remaining chocolate mixture evenly over the marzipan. Return the baking pan to the freezer for at least 2 hours, preferably overnight.

6. Remove baking pan from freezer and flip the pan over. Gently peel off the parchment paper and cut bars into 1-inch squares.

7. Bars can be stored in an airtight container in the refrigerator for up to 5 days.

Cornflake Bars

40

The combination of cornflakes and chocolate is a guaranteed favorite with the kids.

INGREDIENTS

½ cup heavy cream

10 oz. unsweetened chocolate

2 cups cornflakes, or any other cereal of choice

PREPARATION

1. Line the bottom of an 8-inch by 5-inch baking pan with parchment paper (cutting it to fit the bottom of the pan exactly). Preheat oven to 350°F.

2. Heat the heavy cream in a medium saucepan over medium heat until just boiling, and then remove from heat. Using a whisk, stir in the chocolate until mixture is combined and smooth.

3. Pour half of the chocolate mixture into the prepared baking pan and place in freezer for 10 minutes.

4. Remove from freezer and evenly sprinkle one cup of the cornflakes on top of the chocolate that has been in the freezer. Pour the remaining chocolate mixture over the cornflakes and then sprinkle on the remaining cornflakes. Place the baking pan in the freezer for at least 2 hours, preferably overnight.

5. Remove baking pan from freezer and flip the pan over. Gently peel off the parchment paper and cut bars into 1-inch squares.

6. Bars can be stored in an airtight container in the refrigerator for up to 5 days.

Granola Bars

40

Make these with good quality organic granola, or even try your own homemade granola recipe, and you will taste the difference.

INGREDIENTS

½ cup heavy cream

10 oz. unsweetened chocolate

1 cup granola

¼ cup honey

½ stick (2 oz.) butter, melted

PREPARATION

1. Line the bottom of an 8-inch by 5-inch baking pan with parchment paper (cutting it to fit the bottom of the pan exactly). Preheat oven to 350°F.

2. Heat the heavy cream in a medium saucepan over medium heat until just boiling, and then remove from heat. Using a whisk, stir in the chocolate until mixture is combined and smooth.

3. Place the granola, honey and melted butter in a large bowl and mix until well combined.

4. Place the granola on the bottom of the prepared baking pan and use your fingers to press it down to create an even, packed layer. Pour the chocolate mixture over the granola. Place the baking pan in the freezer for at least 2 hours, preferably overnight.

5. Remove baking pan from freezer and flip the pan over. Gently peel off the parchment paper and cut bars into 1-inch squares.

6. Bars can be stored in an airtight container in the refrigerator for up to 5 days.

Crispy Chocolate Chip Squares

Makes

40

It only takes three ingredients to make these fabulous little treats, which will delight anyone who enters your kitchen.

INGREDIENTS

½ cup heavy cream

10 oz. unsweetened chocolate

¾ cup dark chocolate chips

PREPARATION

1. Line the bottom of an 8-inch by 5-inch baking pan with parchment paper (cutting it to fit the bottom of the pan exactly).

2. Heat the heavy cream in a medium saucepan over medium heat until just boiling, and then remove from heat. Using a whisk, stir in the chocolate until mixture is combined and smooth.

3. Pour half of the chocolate mixture into the prepared baking pan and place in freezer for 10 minutes.

4. After 10 minutes, remove the baking pan from the freezer and sprinkle the chocolate chips evenly over the chocolate mixture. Pour the remaining chocolate mixture evenly over the chocolate chips. Return the baking pan to the freezer for at least 2 hours, preferably overnight.

5. Remove baking pan from freezer and flip the pan over. Gently peel off the parchment paper and cut bars into 1-inch squares.

6. Bars can be stored in an airtight container in the refrigerator for up to 5 days.

Chocolate Blondie Squares

Makes

40

Your favorite blondie just got upgraded with an additional layer of chocolate.

INGREDIENTS

1½ sticks (6 oz.) butter

1 cup brown sugar

1 egg

1 teaspoon pure vanilla extract

½ teaspoon baking powder

¼ teaspoon baking soda

1 cup all-purpose flour

¼ cup chocolate chips

½ cup heavy cream

10 oz. unsweetened chocolate

PREPARATION

1. Line the bottom of an 8-inch by 5-inch baking pan with parchment paper (cutting it to fit the bottom of the pan exactly). Preheat oven to 350°F.

2. Using a mixer fitted with a whisk attachment, mix together the butter and brown sugar on medium speed for 3 minutes, until the mixture is smooth. Add the egg and vanilla extract, and mix for another minute.

3. Gradually add the baking powder, baking soda and flour to the mixer, and continue to mix for another 2 minutes until all ingredients are combined.

4. Using a wooden spoon or flexible spatula, stir in the chocolate chips.

5. Pour batter evenly into the prepared baking pan and bake for 22 minutes.

6. Remove from oven and cool on a wire rack for 45 minutes.

7. Meanwhile, prepare the chocolate: Heat the heavy cream in a medium saucepan over medium heat until just boiling, and then remove from heat. Using a whisk, stir in the chocolate until mixture is combined and smooth.

8. Once the blondies have cooled to room temperature, pour the chocolate mixture over the blondies and freeze for at least 2 hours, preferably overnight.

9. Remove baking pan from freezer and flip the pan over. Gently peel off the parchment paper and cut bars into 1-inch squares.

10. Bars can be stored in an airtight container in the refrigerator for up to 5 days.

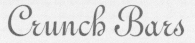

Crunch Bars

Makes

40

Next time you throw a party, save your leftover ice cream cones and make these fabulously crunchy bars.

INGREDIENTS

½ cup heavy cream

10 oz. unsweetened chocolate

1 cup waffle ice cream cone, crumbled

PREPARATION

1. Line the bottom of an 8-inch by 5-inch baking pan with parchment paper (cutting it to fit the bottom of the pan exactly). Preheat oven to 350°F.

2. Heat the heavy cream in a medium saucepan over medium heat until just boiling, and then remove from heat. Using a whisk, stir in the chocolate until mixture is combined and smooth. Add the waffle cone crumbs and use a spoon to mix until combined.

3. Pour the entire mixture into the prepared baking pan and place in the freezer for at least 2 hours, preferably overnight.

5. Remove baking pan from freezer and flip the pan over. Gently peel off the parchment paper and cut bars into 2-inch by 1-inch rectangles.

6. Bars can be stored in an airtight container in the refrigerator for up to 5 days.

Crispy Chocolate and Hazelnut Treats

Makes

12

Chocolate and hazelnuts make for a wonderful pair in this easy-to-make recipe.

INGREDIENTS

½ cup sugar

1 cup blanched hazelnuts, peeled

1 tablespoon canola oil

½ cup heavy cream

10 oz. unsweetened chocolate

PREPARATION

1. Line the bottom of an 8-inch by 5-inch baking pan with parchment paper (cutting it to fit the bottom of the pan exactly).

2. Heat the sugar in a small saucepan over medium heat for about 3-5 minutes, until the sugar melts and turns a light caramel color. Lower the heat and add the hazelnuts. Use a wooden spoon to stir until all the hazelnuts are covered in a layer of caramel. Continue to cook for 3-5 minutes and remove from heat.

3. Spread the canola oil evenly onto a large plate and place the hazelnuts onto the oiled plate. Allow to cook for 45 minutes.

4. Once cooled, place the hazelnuts in a food processor and pulse until the hazelnuts are coarsely chopped (making sure not to fully crush them). Set aside for later use.

5. Heat the heavy cream in a medium saucepan over medium heat until just boiling, and then remove from heat. Using a whisk, stir in the chocolate until mixture is combined and smooth.

6. Pour half of the chocolate mixture into the prepared baking pan and place in freezer for 10 minutes.

7. After 10 minutes, remove the baking pan from the freezer and sprinkle the chopped hazelnuts evenly over the chocolate mixture. Pour the remaining chocolate mixture evenly over the hazelnuts. Return the baking pan to the freezer for at least 2 hours, preferably overnight.

8. Remove baking pan from freezer and flip the pan over. Gently peel off the parchment paper and cut bars into 1-inch squares. Bars can be stored in an airtight container in the refrigerator for up to 5 days.

Chocolate Date Bars

Makes

40

Use Medjool dates for this recipe if you can find them; they are large, sweet and succulent.

INGREDIENTS

½ cup heavy cream

10 oz. unsweetened chocolate

1 tablespoon rum

1 cup dates, pitted and coarsely chopped

PREPARATION

1. Line the bottom of an 8-inch by 5-inch baking pan with parchment paper (cutting it to fit the bottom of the pan exactly).

2. Heat the heavy cream in a medium saucepan over medium heat until just boiling, and then remove from heat. Using a whisk, stir in the chocolate until mixture is combined and smooth. Add the rum and stir to combine.

3. Pour half of the chocolate mixture into the prepared baking pan and place in freezer for 10 minutes.

4. After 10 minutes, remove the baking pan from the freezer and place the chopped dates evenly over the chocolate mixture. Pour the remaining chocolate mixture evenly over the dates. Return the baking pan to the freezer for at least 2 hours, preferably overnight.

5. Remove baking pan from freezer and flip the pan over. Gently peel off the parchment paper and cut bars into 1-inch squares.

6. Bars can be stored in an airtight container in the refrigerator for up to 5 days.

Chocolate and Almond Crispy Treat

20

You can make this recipe using the nut of your choice; just replace the chopped almonds with any other chopped nut, such as walnuts, hazelnuts or pecans.

INGREDIENTS

For the almond layer

½ stick (2 oz.) butter, softened

¾ cup sugar

3 tablespoons all-purpose flour

2 cups almonds, coarsely chopped

3 egg whites

For the chocolate layer

½ cup heavy cream

7 oz. unsweetened chocolate

1 tablespoon almond-flavored liqueur, such as Amaretto

PREPARATION

1. Preheat oven to 325°F. Butter a 12-inch by 8-inch baking pan.

2. **Make the almond layer:** In a large bowl, use a whisk to mix together the butter and sugar until the mixture is smooth. Add the flour and continue to mix. Using a wooden spoon, add the chopped almonds and stir until combined.

3. Using a mixer fitted with a whisk attachment, whisk the egg whites on high speed for about 7 minutes until glossy, white peaks form. Use a rubber spatula to fold the egg whites into the prepared almond batter until combined.

4. Pour the mixture into the prepared baking pan and bake for 25 minutes.

5. Remove from oven and allow to cool on a cooling rack for 1 hour.

6. **Prepare the chocolate layer:** Heat the heavy cream in a medium saucepan over medium heat until just boiling, and then remove from heat. Using a whisk, stir in the chocolate and almond liqueur until mixture is combined and smooth.

7. Pour the prepared chocolate mixture evenly over the almond layer. Place the baking pan in the freezer for at least 2 hours, preferably overnight.

8. Remove baking pan from freezer and flip the pan over. Gently peel off the parchment paper and cut bars into 3-inch by 1-inch rectangles.

9. Bars can be stored in an airtight container in the refrigerator for up to 5 days.

Triple Chocolate Bites

15

Chocolate lovers of all types will adore what these treats have to offer: milk chocolate, white chocolate and dark chocolate; all in one bite.

INGREDIENTS

For the white chocolate layer

4 oz. white chocolate

½ cup hazelnuts, coarsely chopped

For the milk chocolate layer

2 tablespoons heavy cream

3 oz. milk chocolate

For the dark chocolate layer

¼ cup heavy cream

5 oz. unsweetened chocolate

PREPARATION

1. Line the bottom of a 9-inch by 5-inch baking pan with parchment paper (cutting it to fit the bottom of the pan exactly).

2. Make the white chocolate layer: Place the white chocolate in a small microwavable bowl and melt the chocolate in the microwave (making sure not to burn the chocolate). Once melted, use a fork to stir the chocolate until smooth.

3. Sprinkle the chopped hazelnuts evenly on the bottom of the prepared baking pan and then pour the melted white chocolate on top of the nuts. Place baking pan in freezer.

4. Make the milk chocolate layer: Heat the heavy cream and milk chocolate in a medium saucepan over low heat, and use a wooden spoon to stir until the chocolate has melted and the mixture is smooth. Remove the baking pan from the freezer and pour in the milk chocolate mixture evenly. Return pan to freezer.

5. Make the dark chocolate layer: Heat the heavy cream in a medium saucepan over medium heat until just boiling, and then remove from heat. Using a whisk, stir in the chocolate until mixture is combined and smooth.

6. Remove baking pan from freezer and pour in the dark chocolate mixture evenly. Return the baking pan to the freezer for at least 2 hours, preferably overnight.

7. Remove baking pan from freezer and flip the pan over. Gently peel off the parchment paper and cut bars into 3-inch by 1-inch rectangles.

8. Bars can be stored in an airtight container in the refrigerator for up to 5 days.

Chocolate Sable Bars

Makes

12

Sable cookies are French shortbread cookies. These bars take the cookie, add chocolate, and turn them into the most scrumptious little snacks.

INGREDIENTS

For the sable crust

1¼ sticks (5 oz.) butter, very cold and cubed

½ cup powdered sugar

1 egg + 1 egg, beaten (for glazing)

2 tablespoons good quality cocoa powder

1⅔ cups all-purpose flour

½ teaspoon salt

¼ cup sugar

For the chocolate cream layer

¾ cup heavy cream

1 teaspoon pure vanilla extract

8 oz. unsweetened chocolate

PREPARATION

1. **Prepare the sable crust:** Using a mixer fitted with a paddle attachment, mix the butter and powdered sugar together on low speed for 5 minutes, until the mixture is smooth and creamy.

2. Add the egg, cocoa powder and half the flour and continue to mix on low speed for another 2 minutes. Turn off mixer, add the remaining flour and salt, and continue mixing on low speed for another 2 minutes, until the dough is light brown in color and slightly shiny.

3. Remove the dough from the mixer and form a ball. Wrap the dough in plastic wrap and refrigerate for 1 hour.

4. Preheat oven to 350°F.

5. Remove dough from the refrigerator and, working on a lightly floured surface, roll the dough out to a thickness of about an ⅛-inch. Using a sharp knife, cut 3-inch by 1-inch rectangles out of the dough and place on a baking sheet lined with parchment paper.

6. Brush the rectangles with the beaten egg and then generously sprinkle sugar on top of each. Bake for 20 minutes. Allow to chill on cooling rack for at least 40 minutes.

(continued on page 136)

(continued from page 134)

7. **Prepare the chocolate cream layer:** Heat the heavy cream and vanilla extract in a medium saucepan over medium heat until just boiling, and then remove from heat.

8. Using a whisk, stir in the chocolate until mixture is combined and smooth. Place chocolate cream mixture in the freezer for 40 minutes.

9. **Assemble the bars:** Remove the chocolate cream from the freezer. Place 1 leveled tablespoon of the chocolate cream on one sable crust rectangle and cover with another rectangle.

10. Place another tablespoon of chocolate onto the top layer and then top with another sable crust rectangle, making a double-decker sandwich.

11. Bars can be stored in an airtight container in the refrigerator for up to 2 days.

Crispy Chocolate and Almond Fingers

Makes

15

The almond-flavored liqueur in this recipe gives these bars an extra deep almond flavor, without the alcohol aftertaste.

INGREDIENTS

½ cup sugar

1 cup blanched almonds

1 tablespoon canola oil

½ cup heavy cream

10 oz. unsweetened chocolate

2 tablespoons almond-flavored liqueur, such as Amaretto

PREPARATION

1. Line the bottom of a 9-inch by 5-inch baking pan with parchment paper (cutting it to fit the bottom of the pan exactly).

2. Heat the sugar in a small saucepan over medium heat, until the sugar melts and turns a light caramel color. Lower heat and add the almonds. Use a wooden spoon to stir until all the almonds are covered in a layer of caramel. Continue to cook for another 2 minutes and remove from heat.

3. Spread the canola oil evenly onto a large plate and place the almonds onto the oiled plate. Allow to cook for 45 minutes.

4. Once cooled, place the almonds in a food processor and pulse until the almonds are coarsely chopped (making sure not to fully crush them). Set aside for later use.

5. Heat the heavy cream in a medium saucepan over medium heat until just boiling, and then remove from heat. Using a whisk, stir in the chocolate and almond liqueur until mixture is combined and smooth.

6. Pour half of the chocolate mixture into the prepared baking pan and place in freezer for 10 minutes.

7. After 10 minutes, remove the baking pan from the freezer and sprinkle the chopped almonds evenly over the chocolate mixture. Pour the remaining chocolate mixture evenly over the almonds. Return the baking pan to the freezer for at least 2 hours, preferably overnight.

8. Remove baking pan from freezer and flip the pan over. Gently peel off the parchment paper and cut into 3-inch by 1-inch rectangles.

9. Bars can be stored in an airtight container in the refrigerator for up to 5 days.

Chocolate Whisky Squares

Makes

40

Whisky lovers will love this perfect chocolate whisky snack.

INGREDIENTS

½ cup heavy cream

10 oz. unsweetened chocolate

2 tablespoons good quality whisky

PREPARATION

1. Line the bottom of an 8-inch by 5-inch baking pan with parchment paper (cutting it to fit the bottom of the pan exactly).

2. Heat the heavy cream in a medium saucepan over medium heat until just boiling, and then remove from heat. Using a whisk, stir in the chocolate until mixture is combined and smooth. Add the whisky and stir to combine.

3. Pour the chocolate mixture into the prepared baking pan and place in freezer for at least 2 hours, preferably overnight.

4. Remove baking pan from freezer and flip the pan over. Gently peel off the parchment paper and cut bars into 1-inch squares.

5. Bars can be stored in an airtight container in the refrigerator for up to 5 days.

Tips and Tools

TIPS

• Before you start to prepare a recipe, make sure you have read through the entire recipe properly. Check to see if the recipe requires refrigeration or freezing and make sure that you have the required space available in the refrigerator/freezer. Make sure you have the proper pans, tools and ingredients listed. Check to see that you understand each step; if not, read it through until you do.

• Always use the freshest and best quality ingredients, such as whole milk, fresh eggs, alcohol, etc.

• Make sure to preheat the oven as called for in the recipe.

• Use the best quality chocolate you can buy, which contains at least 60% cacao. You can use chocolate that contains 80% cacao, but you should then increase the amount of sugar by ⅓ in order to neutralize the bitterness.

• Always melt chocolate in a bowl placed above a pan filled with simmering water. Make sure that the water doesn't actually touch the bowl. Only mix the chocolate when it has begun to melt.

TOOLS

Baking Pans

Each recipe will stipulate the size and shape of the baking pan you need. These are the basic pans a baker should have on hand:

• Three 8-inch round cake pans

• Springform pans, one 8-inch, one 9-inch, preferably nonstick

• One Bundt pan

• One 12-cup fluted tube pan

• Two 8-inch X 4-inch loaf pans

• One 9-inch tart pan

• Two 8-inch X 10-inch baking pans

• One 8-inch X 12-inch baking pan

I always prefer to use nonstick pans when available.

Measuring Tools

Baking is an exact science and it is important to stick to the amounts listed in the recipes. Therefore, I highly suggest working with measuring devices, such as a digital scale, measuring cups, measuring spoons, a professional baking thermometer, etc. Measuring tools can be bought at nearly all home goods stores.

Oven

Ovens range greatly in functionality and strength; therefore it is important to take your particular oven into consideration when relating to the given baking times.

Pastry Bags and Decorating Tips

Also known as piping bags, pastry bags can be purchased at specialty cooking shops, along with an assortment of matching tips. Decorating tips come in various sizes and shapes, allowing for a vast choice of designs.

Rolling Pin

It is best to use a heavy, smooth, and sturdy rolling pin with a high wood content. Rolling pins can also be made out of marble, stone or plastic, but the wooden ones are preferable, as they can handle the most amounts of excess flour. You should avoid wetting the rolling pin as much as possible. When choosing a rolling pin, keep size in mind; the longer the rolling pin, the more dough it will be able to handle. Always remember to flour both the rolling pin and the working space.

Wire Cooling Rack

Baked goods should be placed on a cooling rack once they are taken out of the oven to allow the air to circulate evenly, thus preventing them from becoming soggy and moist.

Metric Equivalents

The recipes that appear in this cookbook use the standard United States method for measuring liquid and dry or solid ingredients (teaspoons, tablespoons, and cups). The information on this chart is provided to help cooks outside the U.S. successfully use these recipes. All equivalents are approximate.

METRIC EQUIVALENTS FOR DIFFERENT TYPES OF INGREDIENTS

A standard cup measure of a dry or solid ingredient will vary in weight depending on the type of ingredient. A standard cup of liquid is the same volume for any type of liquid. Use the following chart when converting standard cup measures to grams (weight) or milliliters (volume).

Standard Cup	Fine Powder (ex. flour)	Grain (ex. rice)	Granular (ex. sugar)	Liquid Solids (ex. butter)	liquid (ex. milk)
1	140 g	150 g	190 g	200 g	240 ml
¾	105 g	113 g	143 g	150 g	180 ml
⅔	93 g	100 g	125 g	133 g	160 ml
½	70 g	75 g	95 g	100 g	120 ml
⅓	47 g	50 g	63 g	67 g	80 ml
¼	35 g	38 g	48 g	50 g	60 ml
⅛	18 g	19 g	24 g	25 g	30 ml

USEFUL EQUIVALENTS FOR DRY INGREDIENTS BY WEIGHT

(To convert ounces to grams, multiply the number of ounces by 30.)

1 oz	=	¹⁄₁₆ lb	=	30 g
4 oz	=	¼ lb	=	120 g
8 oz	=	½ lb	=	240 g
12 oz	=	¾ lb	=	360 g
16 oz	=	1 lb	=	480 g

USEFUL EQUIVALENTS FOR LENGTH

(To convert inches to centimeters, multiply the number of inches by 2.5.)

1 in				=	2.5 cm		
6 in	=	½ ft		=	15 cm		
12 in	=	1 ft		=	30 cm		
36 in	=	3 ft	=	1 yd	=	90 cm	
40 in				=	100 cm	=	1 m

USEFUL EQUIVALENTS FOR DRY INGREDIENTS BY WEIGHT

¼ tsp			=	1 ml
½ tsp			=	2 ml
1 tsp			=	5 ml
3 tsp =	1 tbls		½ fl oz =	15 ml
	2 tbls =	⅛ cup =	1 fl oz =	30 ml
	4 tbls =	¼ cup =	2 fl oz =	60 ml
	5 ⅓ tbls =	⅓ cup =	3 fl oz =	80 ml
	8 tbls =	½ cup =	4 fl oz =	120 ml
	10 ⅔ tbls =	⅔ cup =	5 fl oz =	160 ml
	12 tbls =	¾ cup =	6 fl oz =	180 ml
	16 tbls =	1 cup =	8 fl oz =	240 ml
	1 pt =	2 cups =	16 fl oz =	480 ml
	1 qt =	4 cups =	32 fl oz =	960 ml
		=	33 fl oz =	1000 ml = 1 liter

USEFUL EQUIVALENTS FOR COOKING/OVEN TEMPERATURES

	Fahrenheit	Celsius	Gas Mark
Freeze Water	32° F	0° C	
Room Temperature	68° F	20° C	
Boil Water	212° F	100° C	
Bake	325° F	160° C	3
	350° F	180° C	4
	375° F	190° C	5
	400° F	200° C	6
	425° F	220° C	7
	450° F	230° C	8
Broil			Grill

Index